"When *Dirty Dancing* showed up on cable, I watched it only half-heartedly, but Andrea Warner's *The Time of My Life* brilliantly explains how wrong I was. With memoir, music criticism, reception theory, and feminist politics, she foregrounds how vital a movie this was and especially (but not only) how its depiction of abortion and bodily autonomy has today become even more radical."
— Steacy Easton, critic and author of *Why Tam͞*   *te Matters* and *Daddy Lessons*

"Andrea Warner is a gift to pop cul͞
The Time of My Life is even mor͞
    and thoughtful analysis, W͞   ͞y
Dancing is more than a lo͞   ͞umph,
                    just like
        — Anne T. Donahue, a͞   ͞y Cares

"I had the time of my life reading Andrea's smart, funny, and insightful take on *Dirty Dancing*. Meticulously researched, this book expertly explains how *Dirty Dancing* is more than just a dance film or a love story. Like Baby, this book should never be put in a corner."
— Lisa Whittington-Hill, author of *Girls, Interrupted*

"What Andrea Warner has achieved here is masterful: taking an iconic cultural touchstone and inviting readers into a timeless conversation on how it marked not only her own life, but also our collective hearts. *The Time of My Life* is heartbreaking and sweet, thoughtful and radical."
— Niko Stratis, culture writer

the pop classics series

the time of my life.

dirty dancing

andrea warner

ecwpress

Editor for the press: Jen Sookfong Lee
Copy editor: Jen Knoch
Cover and text design: David Gee

Library and Archives Canada Cataloguing
in Publication

Title: The time of my life : Dirty dancing /
Andrea Warner.

Names: Warner, Andrea, author.

Series: Pop classic series ; #13.

Description: Series statement: Pop classics ; 13

Identifiers: Canadiana (print)
20230567894 | Canadiana (ebook)
20230567932

ISBN 978-1-77041-741-0 (softcover)
ISBN 978-1-77852-267-3 (ePub)
ISBN 978-1-77852-268-0 (PDF)

Subjects: LCSH: Dirty dancing (Motion
picture) | LCSH: Ardolino, Emile—Criticism
and interpretation.

Classification: LCC PN1997.D57 W37
2024 | DDC 791.43/72—dc23

Printing: Friesens   5 4 3 2 1
PRINTED AND BOUND IN CANADA

This book is funded in part by the Government of Canada. Ce livre est financé en partie par le
gouvernement du Canada. We acknowledge the support of the Canada Council for the Arts.
Nous remercions le Conseil des arts du Canada de son soutien. We acknowledge the funding
support of the Ontario Arts Council (OAC), an agency of the Government of Ontario. We also
acknowledge the support of the Government of Ontario through the Ontario Book Publishing
Tax Credit, and through Ontario Creates.

Justice for every Penny we've ever lost and love to every Penny who survived. Abortion is healthcare and everybody deserves access to safe abortions.

Contents

Introduction

I first saw *Dirty Dancing* when I was nine years old, about six months after it was released. It came out in the summer of 1987, and I didn't see it in a theater, of course. Movies were expensive and it was a rare treat to actually go watch something on the big screen. The movie was rated PG-13 and my parents were cool but not *that* cool. Keeping up with the pop culture zeitgeist was not their priority; we were a family that waited for the VHS release, and even then most of our home video screenings came courtesy of visits to our maternal grandparents' house and the young uncles and aunt who still lived at home and were constantly renting a rotation of videos. They didn't care if we watched with them, so this was how my sister, Jenn, and I ended up sitting on the carpet in front of the television Sunday after Sunday watching things like *Mannequin* and *Ferris Bueller's Day Off* and, eventually, *Dirty Dancing*. When I ask Jenn, who is 13 months younger than me, what she recalls from that first viewing, memories tumble out. "Oh my god! It was *soooo* awkward because it was so sexy and everyone

1

was in the room with us. I was dying." It's the kind of moment you can't know is embarrassing until it's happening to you, but you never forget it. The first multigenerational family movie screening that ends up playing a small part in your sexual awakening? They don't make a mug for that, but they should.

I remember the discomfort of watching this with my family: it felt like I'd swallowed some kind of twin nightmare, a lava monster full of hormones accompanied by an ice-cold anxiety ghost. I was queasy and afraid of the rush in my body that I was certain everyone could see. What if my aunt and uncles drew attention to us watching this, laughing at us squirming in our seats? What if my parents or grandparents overheard and walked into the room? What if they said we were too young and turned off the television? I held my breath and felt the blush crawl up my cheeks, feeling sick and thrilled simultaneously.

It wasn't like *Dirty Dancing* was the first time I'd felt stirred by sexy content, either. I had been watching euphemistic sex scenes on soap operas for years already, and I was an early devotee of Miss Piggy's overt and unapologetic lust. My childhood best friend and I put my Barbies through all kinds of pseudo-sexual situations, rubbing smooth plastic crotches against smooth plastic crotches in a slippery frenzy, not understanding each stroke was supposed to build toward release. We just did it until our hands tired. These recreations didn't just stem from what we were watching in movies, or hearing about in pop music, or watching on TV or in music videos. My best friend's mom used to write love notes on her daughter's behalf and make her bring them to a boy in our kindergarten class. Fellow grade-schoolers started having little boyfriend and girlfriend relationships in Grade 1 or 2. Family members would ask us if we had crushes on anybody at school, or if anybody had crushes on us. We'd tease each other about Michael J. Fox and Malcolm-Jamal Warner being our imaginary boyfriends. We were primed, ready, and waiting for something like *Dirty Dancing* to come along.

I saw *Footloose* and *Flashdance* in that living room, too. My teenaged and young adult aunt and uncles weren't just obsessed with intensely choreographed dance movies exploring class, morality, and sex; this continual rotation of films was how the younger members of the family found some common bond. It was a way for all of us to be together, even if sometimes we felt discomfort. But it was the dance movies that really stood out to me. In my head and heart, I loved to dance. I didn't want to take lessons or work at it, but I loved dancing in my room or with my sister and friends. I also loved the idea of what it could represent.

Even by the age of nine, I had already been told over and over, explicitly and implicitly, that my fat-since-birth body was "bad." The messaging from some family, most of society, and pop culture was that my fat body was a social ill and sign of excess, a moral failing, a lack of control and discipline, and that I wasn't being properly cared for. I did not appear to sufficiently hate myself (or love myself, depending on who was talking),

and doctors, family members, strangers, and friends were baf-
fled, angry, ashamed, and maybe even jealous that I could not
be trimmed, halved, or lessened. Dancing wasn't supposed to be
for a body like mine, so it felt subversive to engage in rhythmic
movement. But it wasn't just a radical act; it was joyful and it
was freeing.

When I was in Grade 4, my sister and I spent hours in
my friend's basement creating choreography for our dance and
lip sync performance to Cyndi Lauper's "Girls Just Want to
Have Fun" in front of our entire elementary school. When
my nephew was three and lived down the hall from me and my
husband, they would come over most nights for a dance party.
When I was 41, in the first year of the pandemic, I tried some
learn-to-dance choreo videos on YouTube. It wasn't as much
fun as just putting on music and letting my body find its own
expression, but it was still a good time. Dance is the one
activity where I gleefully chose to move my body and inhabit
my body for *me*; it was never the gymnastic classes or the ice
skating, badminton, and swimming lessons that I attended
regularly as a child. Dance movies made deliberate movement
look fun and cool in a way that nothing else ever did. Dancing
could be a form of rebellion, a gateway to sexy times, or a path
to express myself in a world that usually wanted to shut me
up. Before I ever fully grasped the concept of metaphor, these
films helped me understand dance as resistance, as joy, and as
feminist embodiment.

In *Flashdance*, Alex is a 19-year-old welder by day and cabaret dancer by night. She dreams of dancing professionally,

of melding ballet and contemporary dance in a "respectable" institution that will help her transcend her blue-collar day job and her after-hours work as an exotic dancer (which, in the world of this movie, is implied to be the lowest class of dance because of its proximity to sex work). Dance is a place to dream of something bigger and better, as well as an art and talent and skill to be commodified. Alex's style of dance is coded as being "cheapened" by the sexiness of the performance, no matter how much incredible creativity she displays with her show-stopping routines. She performs a stunning piece of choreography in the club with just a chair and more water than is probably safe for an indoor stage show using that much electricity. The men in the audience — and it's all men — leer and whistle when she finishes. This is not the ballet, the scene screams, this is not high art. This is sex work. I'm not saying I understood the nuances and complexities of *Flashdance* when I was nine, but I did see how dance was complicated for Alex, and I was fascinated that it could be so many things to her. She wanted to be a dancer, but dance was also a place of tension, creativity, catharsis, joy, shame, and escape.

In *Footloose*, dance becomes a symbol for everything. Ren, a big-city high-school senior, rolls into a small, devout town ruled with an iron fist by a grief-stricken pastor. Ren learns that dancing has been banned in the town, which means the graduating class can't have a prom. He rallies some pals and protests the decision, making an impassioned speech at a town meeting and invoking passages from the bible that specifically glorify dance. Ren's rejection of the seemingly arbitrary and unfair dance ban had a direct impact on me and my friends when our elementary-school principal decided to abolish our Grade 7 grad dance. The "reasons" she gave at the time seemed flimsy and lightly fascist to my 13-year-old self, though I no longer remember what they were. I was furious. At the beginning of the school year, she also dissolved student government (I was a devoted student council member), so most of us already didn't care for her. Canceling the dance was our breaking point. So we organized. Some of my classmates and I, with the help of our parents, held our own grad dance in the community center across the lawn from our elementary school. We planned it specifically for a school-day afternoon and all of us would just refuse to come back from lunch. We raised funds through car washes and probably a bake sale, and our parents helped us rent the community center gym. Almost every graduate was there when we filed in, and although we didn't have the kind of choreographed fancy-feet explosion that *Footloose* had, we danced our pre-teen butts off as if we'd won a MuchMusic video dance party.

But it's *Dirty Dancing* that changed my world. It's *Dirty Dancing* that helped shape my burgeoning feminism, made me a lifelong activist for abortion rights, and introduced me to the power of music. It's *Dirty Dancing* that I've returned to over and over and over again, that I've shared with groups of strangers and younger generations in my family and best friends, that I've watched on screens big and small, in cinemas, on dorm-room televisions, iPhones, and the backs of airplane seats.

Dirty Dancing, set in 1963, tells the story of a teenaged girl called Baby who goes on summer vacation with her family. She's meant to start college in the fall and dreams of joining the Peace Corps, and she can't imagine meeting a young man who's better than the father she idolizes. But over the course of a few weeks, Baby's whole privileged world is upended: she meets dance instructor Johnny; has a major sexual awakening; lies to her dad so she can pay for an illicit abortion for her new friend, Penny, then helps save Penny's life when there are complications from said abortion; witnesses in real time that the hypocrisies of the world aren't far away but happening right in front of her, and that she and her family are complicit in them; and works really hard and transforms herself from rhythmically challenged to a passably professional dancer. Baby grows up before our eyes and the movie stays with her every step of her journey, always prioritizing her coming of age as valid, important, and worthy.

Baby, Penny, and *Dirty Dancing* came along and fortified aspects of my values, ethics, and identity that are still core to who I am more than 35 years later: feminism (though more intersectional and inclusive than just what's onscreen here); abortion rights; mutual aid, confronting class divisions and stereotypes; navigating familial obligation and expectation;

helping to dismantle systems of inequity; light crime-solving; the hard work that goes into learning a skill; my deep appreciation for incredible music as well as some not incredible music that benefited from excellent film placement; and, of course, sexual agency for everybody and every body, but especially young women, because there is still so much stigma attached to their pleasure and autonomy.

Scan the trailer or skim the surface of *Dirty Dancing* and it *should* have been a throwaway summer fling film. Instead, it's become an iconic piece of pop culture. In part, the film's ubiquity has helped grow its place in the zeitgeist — it has aired on cable pretty much weekly since I was a teenager — but its endurance isn't just its ubiquity. It's the quotable lines that everyone knows whether they've seen the movie or not. It's the brilliant use of music from the '50s, '60s, '70s, and '80s, even though the film is set in 1963. It's the charm of its cast and the real-life tension and affection between Jennifer Grey and Patrick Swayze surfacing in their excellent performances as Baby and Johnny. It's the erotic heat of Grey's and Swayze's bodies moving in tandem as Baby and Johnny find their rhythm together.

It's also the evocative and risqué title that promises one thing and then delivers so much more. The words *Dirty Dancing* give the first impression, and it's a clever one, because it allows the film itself to tell much bigger stories. There is authenticity at the film's foundation: writer and producer Eleanor Bergstein took inspiration from her own life when she wrote the screenplay. A former dancer who spent summer vacations at Jewish resorts in the Catskills with her family, Bergstein poured aspects of herself, her sister, and other people in her orbit into the characters of Baby, Johnny, Penny, and Baby's sister, Lisa. Bergstein also fought to ensure the film never lost the real-life stakes that subversively drive all of the action, because at its core *Dirty Dancing* is an abortion movie. Penny's need for an abortion is what drives Baby to step into herself in a whole new way, a feminist act of community care that we don't see enough of anywhere in film. It's powerful and resonant, and this sisterhood solidarity is a fascinating counterpoint to the tension and conflict between biological sisters Baby and Lisa, who are initially at odds with each other. Lisa cares about clothes and makeup and Baby reads books. Baby is their father's clear favorite until she eventually, inevitably, disappoints him, much to Lisa's delight. But as Baby and Lisa come to learn each other's secrets, they begin to understand more about the world and themselves.

This might be the real reason *Dirty Dancing* endures: it portrays girls and women as full individuals, and treats its characters and its audiences accordingly. Their grievances and feelings and experiences aren't trivialized, dismissed, or ignored. They are the whole reason *Dirty Dancing* exists. I may not have been able to articulate this when I was nine, but I felt it. Now, as a 44-year-old, I can chart how *Dirty Dancing* helped set me up for a life where I refused to settle for anything less than being the author of my own story; a complete person with agency and purpose and gut instincts that I can trust even if the patriarchy or internalized misogyny or anything else tries to dissuade me from the confidence of my own bones.

Over the course of two weeks in *Dirty Dancing*, we witness Frances "Baby" Houseman's personal journey from gawky, bookish, wannabe savior who doesn't know the foxtrot from the merengue (neither did I) to confident, brilliant, emerging feminist who can nail a tango with gumption and intensive toil. Baby confronts her own naivete, puts her theoretical activism into practice, and evolves from klutz with two left feet to graceful, accomplished, semi-pro dancer. Two weeks change her life and make her part of a de facto community where everybody is better for their time together.

But Baby not only helps other people, she also helps herself. She asks for what she wants and she stands up for what's right; she's vulnerable, brave, and empowered. She's feeling herself in a way she'd never imagined was available to her. Two weeks of transformation to fully realize who she has always been.

Baby's journey was a kind of permission: to seek pleasure, gratification, and joy in my body; to stand up for other people and what I think is right; to revel in the moment, go after what I want, and not be afraid of the next iteration of myself, even if it defies others' expectations. And finally, to not be afraid to have fun. Walt Whitman may have coined the phrase "I contain multitudes," but *Dirty Dancing* — that summer fling, class-conflict romantic dance flick with complex women characters — truly embodies the concept.

1

Be My Baby

"I carried a watermelon."

On the page it probably didn't read like an iconic line.

It comes just 12 minutes into *Dirty Dancing*. Frances "Baby" Houseman (Jennifer Grey) has just hauled a melon almost half her size up a rickety cliffside staircase, crossing a threshold into an area not meant for her and her wealthy resort-going peers. She's shocked and excited to see how the other half live: crotch-to-crotch in a back-bending dance party, a sea of beautiful, young bodies finding rhythms and positions that Baby has likely only dreamed of. She is enthralled. Then she witnesses the arrival of dance instructor Johnny Castle (Patrick Swayze, wearing the hell out of a perfectly fitted pair of black pants), undulating across the crowded floor in a way that seems inclusive and welcoming, never predacious. When they're introduced, Grey's delivery is perfect. Baby blurts, "I carried a watermelon" instead of "Can I climb you?" Swayze, as Johnny, plays the moment well, pausing just long enough to convey an eye roll without actually moving his eyes. "I carried a watermelon" is the best Baby's sexually short-circuiting brain can do as the blood rushes through her body.

It's been a big day for Baby. As *Dirty Dancing* opens, it's her voice in our ears. We see Baby in the backseat of the family car, playing her part in the American dream, her sister, Lisa (Jane Brucker), beside her, Dad (Dr. Jake Houseman, played by future *Law & Order* fave Jerry Orbach) driving, and Mom (Marjorie Houseman, played by future *Gilmore Girls* icon Kelly Bishop) in the passenger seat. As they make their way to Kellerman's, a Jewish summer resort in the Catskills, Baby's voice-over provides the necessary context: it's the summer of 1963 and there's an air of hope and innocence in Baby's bubble. She's bound for college and wants to join the Peace Corps, and she's reading *Plight of the Peasant* while Lisa studies her own image in a compact mirror. Baby tells the audience that she can't imagine finding a guy as great as her father, and it hasn't yet occurred to her to object to the infantilizing nickname "Baby."

Baby's first day at Kellerman's is the beginning of her "real-world" education. The publicly affable owner of the resort is performatively charming to Dr. Houseman and the family, but behind the scenes Baby witnesses him instructing the Ivy League waiters to romance the young daughters, even "the dogs." She's also introduced to the resort owner's smarmy nephew, Neil Kellerman (Lonny Price), who essentially decides that Baby will be "his girl" while she's at the resort, whether she wants that or not. When they join in the dance after dinner, Baby is intrigued when Johnny and Penny burst in and take to the middle of the dance floor, creating a spectacle with their mesmerizing mambo. Baby watches them, transfixed, and swallows hard as the first flush of arousal sucks all the moisture from the upper half of her body. This hard swallow is awkward and visible, but my mouth still goes dry thinking about this moment and relating back to my own first "real world" stirrings. The delicious intrigue of responding to a sexy situation but not yet fully understanding what that means, or what it could possibly portend, can be a little anxiety-inducing, but also very hot. Especially in Baby's case as the murmurs of disapproval and delight blend throughout the room, half the crowd impressed by Penny and Johnny's display, and the other half clutching their pearls. The Kellerman men convey their displeasure at this display of dexterity from their dance pros, but Baby's mini mambo awakening is complete.

But she's quickly brought back down to earth to be in service to the patriarchy, again, as Neil strong-arms her into being the "volunteer" in the evening's magic show alongside the annoying social director, Stan (Wayne Knight). When Baby goes wandering after dark, it's equal parts desperate escape and reclaiming her autonomy. Her hope is that the night holds something better for her. Cue the sound of rock 'n' roll drifting down from the steep cliff that's home to the staff quarters.

She's hesitant until she sees one of the staff, Billy (Neal Jones), struggling to carry an armful of watermelons up to the party. Baby is cute and nice and, most importantly, a late-summer arrival at Kellerman's. Billy leads her up the stairs and bumps open the doors of a large, barn-like structure with a flourish of his backside and Baby's immersed in a wild feast for the senses. There are strict rules forbidding guests from the off-limits staff quarters where the young workers bust loose after all the guests are tucked into bed. The music is raucous, and young bodies are grinding and moving together, bare arms and legs glistening and almost mocking Baby's modest cardigan. She's overwhelmed at first, and then very quickly intrigued and a little turned on. Grey conveys Baby's rapid processing — disoriented then intrigued then turned on — silently, her eyes struggling to take it all in, apprehension and discomfort in the tension of her face, before finally relaxing a little, her eyes starting to light up as Baby's fear gives way to desire.

Then Baby sees Johnny in his natural habitat for the first time. He and his fellow dance instructor Penny burst through the doors that Baby just walked through, largely unnoticed, and the party immediately ratchets up three notches. The Dance Royalty have arrived and the crowd parts to greet them, a rift in a sea of rhythmic coupling. "That's my cousin, Johnny Castle!" Billy says, pointing to Patrick Swayze, who rolls his hips as he dances his way across the room, white shirt open to his navel and tight black pants hugging his hips. Baby tries to be subtle as she watches Johnny move his body, but she can't help but stare. She's in her late teens, a guest at a summer resort in the Catskills. Johnny, a muscled hunk in his mid-20s and a seeming bad boy, is king of the working-class dancers, gyrating and spinning through a sweaty, summer-kissed, sexed-up crowd of young workers. They're living it up on the dance floor after a long day of catering to the likes of Baby and all the other upper-class guests. This is forbidden territory for Baby, and there's nowhere else she'd rather be.

Baby is noticeably excited by Johnny, swallowing hard and staring lustfully, but also by the scene around her. The promise of sex, implied by the titular dirtiness of the dancing, is there, but it's pantomime. The frenzy is as much about the release of bodies moving and skin touching as it is about the wild music and physical abandon taking place in such close proximity to the regimented performance of approved family-friendly activities at the resort. There is freedom in shaking off the stiff rules and class confines, liberation in every beat and thrust.

She has crossed into another world, a world that she imme-diately recognizes as more "real" than the relatively privileged class bubble in which she's been raised. Baby understands blue-collar labor ideologically, but she's likely never meaning-fully engaged with any blue-collar workers. She doesn't fully appreciate that work is an essential means of survival — yet. Through her accidental eavesdropping, Baby already has a better understanding of the class differences within the resort and the hierarchy of the staff. Up until this moment, Baby's engagement with the "real" world has been hypothetical. She has her eyes set on the Peace Corps. Anti-war protests are already starting against the conflict in Vietnam, even though America has not admitted that a war is occurring. The Civil Rights Movement is demanding equality and being met with deliberate acts of anti-Black violence and white supremacist terrorism. These aren't specifically named in the film, but they're acknowledged. When Baby is introduced to the owner of Kellerman's as someone who is going to "change the world," she receives a pat on the head from her father, a gesture that reads as proud and more than a little condescending. The threat of Baby's burgeoning agency is foreshadowed.

At the staff party, Johnny finally takes note of Baby's existence, not as a love interest or even an object of interest, but because Baby is so out of place. He approaches and we can see Baby's flustered feelings get the better of her as Grey plays up Baby's awkwardness, her mouth slightly agape, her eyes panicked but excited at being perceived by him, the rest of her body frozen. Johnny asks his cousin what Baby's doing there, and Billy vouches for her, proudly stating, "She's with me!" All Baby can say in her own defense is "I carried a watermelon." Grey plays this as Baby briefly leaving her body from the humiliation, repeating the sentence to herself as Johnny walks away, incredulous, Baby's eyes and head down in frustrated embarrassment. But Baby doesn't just slink away after her watermelon gaffe; she stands her ground and tries to sway to the music. When Johnny finally beckons Baby off the sidelines with a "c'mere" gesture, she is hesitant yet eager as he teaches her to ride his thigh. Baby's hips take a few tries to find the right motion, but eventually she gets the hang of it and starts to move with abandon, head thrown back, eyes closed, elated and satisfied. Even when the music drops out and Johnny vanishes, Baby is still dancing, delighted and delirious from this carnal milestone.

Something huge has shifted for Baby and the audience, though, in the wake of this brief walk on the wild side. Grey's performance of Baby's awkwardness is so endearing and the writing so perfect and so squarely entrenched in Baby's perspective that we can't help but relate. Who among us hasn't fumbled our first encounters with people we're desperate to impress? "I carried a watermelon" is the first universal moment in *Dirty Dancing*. Baby and Johnny's interaction isn't a meet-cute — it's a meet-tragicomic, and it is all of us.

Dirty Dancing isn't just another fun but forgettable flick about a summer romance. It's a movie from the point of view of a young woman, a teenaged girl who is to be taken seriously and afforded the majority of the action. Baby is an interesting and real protagonist, cute but not impossibly glamorous in simple dresses, jeans, t-shirts, and white Keds. She isn't a perfect, flawless beauty or a damsel in distress or a girl desperately seeking her identity and worth in the arms of a boy. Baby is smart and principled and a bit naive, but she's also hopeful, honest, and brave. Baby is lust-struck initially, but even in that moment her desire isn't just about Johnny. It's never just about Johnny. There's something in Penny that captures Baby's interest, too: she's a gifted dancer, she seems confident, and she's beautiful. There is also something in this room full of people not much older than her, but who seem to have already found their people and created a community where they know how to dance and be in their bodies, and how to be free and confident in a way that has eluded Baby so far. Baby is ready to have her eyes opened to different worlds, eager for a change and to be changed, to grow up and into future iterations of herself.

Baby is a different kind of hero than is traditionally depicted onscreen, particularly as embodied by young women characters in 1987. *Some Kind of Wonderful* tackles social hierarchy and class in a high school setting. But the protagonist is working-class teen Keith (Eric Stoltz), even if the most memorable character is his best friend, drummer Watts (Mary Stuart Masterson), a gender-nonconforming hero for the masses. *Can't Buy Me Love*'s Cindy (Amanda Peterson) is a popular cheerleader who agrees to pretend to date Reggie (Patrick Dempsey), a nerd, for one month to give him the social status he desperately wants. We get glimpses of Cindy's point of view, but the film is really about Reggie. Neither of these movies prioritize the points of view of their young women characters the way *Dirty Dancing* does. The film belongs to Baby in almost every way. And it is all thanks to the two women who created Baby and brought her to fruition so vividly: Jennifer Grey and screenwriter/producer Eleanor Bergstein, who is, at least in part, a little bit Baby.

THE ORIGINAL BABY

She may not have carried a watermelon in her real life, but the Eleanor Bergstein story *is* the story of *Dirty Dancing*.

Sort of.

Bergstein grew up "dirty dancing" and became a teenage mambo queen. (*I Was a Teenage Mambo Queen* was also one of the suggested alternate titles in case *Dirty Dancing* didn't fly.) Her father was a doctor and her older sister was named Frances (Baby's real name). The family vacationed in the Catskills at Jewish summer resorts like Kellerman's, where Bergstein spent her time taking dance lessons — and winning the resort's dance competitions — while her parents golfed. Bergstein was called "Baby" until she was 22.

Bergstein's reality informs every aspect of the fictional film, which might be why the movie sticks the proverbial landing so well and still resonates more than three decades later. "There's not a second in it that isn't in some way part of my life and my history, but I'm in all the characters, as most writers are," Bergstein told *Gender Across Borders*[1] in 2010. "Everything about it I hope is truthful, and a great deal of it came from particular elements of my life. But, you know, that's different from saying I sat down to write my 17th summer."

It wasn't her 17th summer, but *Dirty Dancing*'s characters, plots, choreography, and music all trace back to Bergstein. Born in 1938, Bergstein grew up in New York City, in a Brooklyn neighborhood she has characterized as rough. The kids around her had a toughness to them, she's said, but that didn't mean they couldn't dance. Bergstein honed her skills under the older youth, winning amateur dance contests in their preferred style: the

---

1 Carrie Polansky, "An Interview with Eleanor Bergstein: On Dirty Dancing, Feminism and the Film Industry," *Gender Across Borders*, May 25, 2010, https://genderacrossborders .wordpress.com/2010/05/25/an-interview-with-eleanor-bergstein-on-dirty-dancing-feminism -and-the-film-industry/.

so-called dirty dancing. "We did this very, very erotic dancing to this rhythm and blues and early rock music, and then we sat in a car and looked at Manhattan, where we thought everybody had sex," Bergstein said in an interview with Yahoo Entertainment.[2] She spent her summers at family resorts like Kellerman's, learning Latin dances and winning more dance contests. Bergstein eventually became a dance teacher at an Arthur Murray studio, which helped pay her way through college.

In 1973, Bergstein debuted her gift for eye-catching titles, publishing her first novel, *Advancing Paul Newman*. The subtitle promises "a story of two liberated women looking for love" while the blurb above the title calls it "the ultra-novel about 'sex in the sixties.'" The liberated women are best friends Kitsy and Ila, both of whom are aspiring writers who travel, have sex (good and bad), and volunteer for the 1968 presidential campaign for the anti-war candidate Eugene McCarthy. This is where the novel takes its title: one of Kitsy and Ila's jobs on the campaign trail is to get the crowds amped up for Newman, who is making appearances in support of McCarthy. *New York Times* reviewer Anatole Broyard praised Bergstein's "nerve" but declared that "because it throbs with largely undirected energy and talent," reading the book was an "exhausting experience." Broyard's review is condescending, paternalistic, and patronizing, and,

2 Gwynne Watkins, "Flashback: 'Dirty Dancing' Screenwriter on Casting Patrick Swayze and That Abortion Plot Line," Yahoo Entertainment, January 27, 2017, https://www.yahoo.com /entertainment/dirty-dancing-screenwriter-on-casting-patrick-swayze-and-that-abortion -plot-line-195621205.html.

of course, revealing of the critic. He refers dismissively to one of Ila's subplots as "a wanton waste of fictional and geographical space" and rejects the authenticity of a group of young people excitedly coming together to affect change. In 1968. "It may be a blind spot on my part, a charley horse of temporary cynicism — or it could be the way Miss Bergstein presents it — but I find it difficult to believe in the 'idealism' of all those volunteers."[3]

Writing in the *Paris Review*, a year ahead of the book's 50th anniversary, poet, essayist, and fiction writer Elisa Gonzalez credited Broyard's "dismissive" review and "his grating conde-scension" for spurring her to read Bergstein's novel. Gonzalez says it's "one of the best minor rebellions I've ever under-taken." According to Gonzalez, *"Advancing Paul Newman* is not simply a story of friendship, albeit one between two com-plicated women. The book is also gorgeously deranged and witty, told in fragments and leaps."[4]

Bergstein continued flexing her gift for writing fully real-ized women characters with agency in her first screenplay, 1980's *It's My Turn.* Starring Jill Clayburgh in the lead role, *It's My Turn's* trailer describes the film as a "funny love story" but the sexy instrumental music is straight out of a soft-core satire. Main character Kate has the "perfect" life — from the right job and clothes to the right relationship with the perfect man — but she's bored. She heads to New York to interview for a

3 Antatole Broyard, "Lost Causes and Characters," *New York Times*, November 27, 1973, https://www.nytimes.com/1973/11/27/archives/lost-causes-and-characters-books-of-the-times-strangers-the-morning.html.

4 Elisa Gonzalez, "On Liberated Women Looking for Love," *The Paris Review*, May 6, 2022, https://www.theparisreview.org/blog/2022/05/06/on-liberated-women-looking-for-love/.

new job and to attend the wedding of her widowed father. She stumbles into a fling with her married, soon-to-be stepbrother who is the absolute embodiment of the wrong man. Enter, as always, Michael Douglas, who excels at embodying variations on that theme, especially in the '80s and '90s (*Fatal Attraction, Wall Street, Basic Instinct, A Perfect Murder*).

It's My Turn didn't make much of a splash at the time — Bergstein's script was even nominated for a Razzie, the yearly awards that "celebrate" the worst of Hollywood cinema — but Bergstein was soon working on her new screenplay. She had written an erotic dance scene for *It's My Turn* that was ultimately cut from the final film, but she taught the crew some hot dance moves in between takes. A couple years later, as Bergstein told the *Philadelphia Inquirer*, she ran into one of the crew members on the street. "He said, 'I remember when you taught us all how to dirty-dance.'"[5] Bergstein saw potential for a new film, and she immediately dug out her old 45 records and got to work. She picked out song after song and played DJ in her living room for her friends and family, essentially recreating the dance parties of her youth. If people were up on their feet immediately, unable to stop themselves from shaking and quaking their bodies, she labelled the song a "priority recording." The music came first, Bergstein told the *Philadelphia Inquirer*, then she "dreamed through the story."[6]

5 Carrie Rickey, "'Dirty Dancing': Panned as a Dud, but Dynamite," *The Inquirer*, August 19, 2012, https://web.archive.org/web/20200607175137/https://www.inquirer.com/philly/entertainment/20120819_Dirty_Dancing___Panned_as_a_dud__but_dynamite.html.

6 Rickey.

Bergstein wanted to ground the film in a certain kind of liberal political idealism that she strongly identified with her own experiences of youth. She decided on the summer of 1963, which to her represented a vital turning point in the culture. It was the summer after the Cuban Missile Crisis. Dr. Reverend Martin Luther King Jr. led the March on Washington for civil rights and delivered his historic "I Have a Dream" speech. Young people were leading the anti-war movement, there was a burgeoning second-wave feminism movement, and the sexual revolution was on the horizon. Bergstein remembers it as a pivotal time of hope, and, in a way, innocence — a cultural "before" to the major socio-political upheaval that followed months later.

"I meant *Dirty Dancing* to be a celebration of the time of your life when you could believe that a kind of earnest, liberal action could remake the world in your own image," Bergstein told the *New York Times* in 1987.[7]

The film couldn't have been set a few months earlier or later. The summer of 1963 was the first one after the Cuban missile crisis, which everyone had been following on television. The effect on kids was to make them very scared, and, for the first time, very suspicious of their elders: maybe things wouldn't work out all right. But the thing that kept the optimism going was John Kennedy

7 Samuel G. Freedman, "A Film That Rocks to an Innocent Beat," *New York Times*, August 16, 1987, https://www.nytimes.com/1987/08/16/movies/film-dirty-dancing-rocks-to-an-innocent-beat.html.

himself — young and energetic and sexy. So maybe you could have it all. It was the summer of the Peace Corps and the summer of the "I Have a Dream" speech. It was like the last summer of liberalism. Because two months after the movie is over, J.F.K. is assassinated. And two months after that the Beatles are on *The Ed Sullivan Show*. And after that, it's radical action.

"I'm always very anxious to be in those moments just before transition," Bergstein later told *Gender Across Borders*.

I was enormously interested in bringing back that time, both politically and socially in America, when everybody really believed that the world had been made safe by World War II, and the only thing left to do was to make it safe for everybody, so the large Jewish community gave lots and lots of money to SNCC [Student Nonviolent Coordinating Committee] and CORE [Congress of Racial Equality] and supported the Freedom Riders, and Martin Luther King made his speech that summer in 1963.[8]

Named after First Lady Eleanor Roosevelt, a lifelong civil rights activist and humanitarian, Bergstein had also been involved in liberal politics her whole life and says the most important thing is to try to make the world better. "This is a

8 Polansky.

classic Jewish value," Bergstein told *Tablet Magazine*, and it accurately reflects the values of the real Jewish resort, Grossinger's, that inspired *Dirty Dancing*'s fictional Kellerman's. Bergstein describes Grossinger as "ethically and morally committed"[9] and remembers Grossinger giving a eulogy when MLK was assassinated in 1968 and holding candlelight vigils in honor of murdered civil rights workers.

The invisible backstory Bergstein conceived as the framework for *Dirty Dancing* was that this summer vacation has an ulterior motive. The Housemans' trip coincides with the March on Washington, where M.L.K. will deliver his iconic speech. Baby wants to be there, but Dr. and Mrs. Houseman, as liberal as they are in theory, want to keep their daughter far away from the frontlines of the actual Civil Rights Movement. They whisk her off on this family vacation that proves life-changing in very different ways. *Dirty Dancing* had to happen at this moment, Bergstein said, because it was the last summer "you felt like you could reach out your hand and change the world."[10]

Dr. Houseman echoes part of this sentence when he introduces Baby at Kellerman's, a fatherly mixture of pride, affection, and patronizing head-patting as he declares "our Baby's going to change the world." In her 2010 *Jezebel* essay "Dirty Dancing Is the Greatest Movie of All Time," Irin Carmon describes

9 Sophie Aroesty, "A Conversation with Eleanor Bergstein, Writer and Producer of 'Dirty Dancing,' on its 30th Anniversary," *Tablet Magazine*, August 28, 2017, https://www.tabletmag.com/sections/news/articles/jewcy-dirty-dancing.

10 Andrea Simakis, "Eleanor Bergstein Wants You to Have the Time of Your Life at the Live Stage Version of 'Dirty Dancing,' Now Headed to Cleveland," Cleveland.com, February 28, 2015, https://www.cleveland.com/onstage/2015/02/eleanor_bergstein_wants_you_to.html

Baby "as the daughter of the first generation of American Jews to read widespread upper-middle-class prosperity, if not elite cultural acceptance, she is swathed in a pre-Kennedy assassination liberalism. But her time at Kellerman's that summer is a loss of innocence in one significant way — and I'm not talking about her virginity."

Reinforcing what Baby's been told her whole life — that she can do anything and change the world — Carmon writes that Baby's real wake-up call comes when

> faced with the hypocrisy of a long-shunned minority enacting its own unexamined exclusion, this time on class grounds. The guests at Kellerman's look comfortable, but they were raised in the Depression and traumatized by World War II. She can contrast the welcome her family received at the resort with the chilly, dismissive one Johnny and his working-class dance crew gets. She can dance with the owner's son and thaw a little when she learns he's going freedom riding with the bus boys, then see how he treats Johnny. She can find out that the supposed prize, Yale Medical school and out-WASPing-the-WASPs Robbie, is also an Ayn Rand–reading cad whose life philosophy is, "Some people count, some people don't."[11]

11 Irin Carmon, "*Dirty Dancing* Is the Greatest Movie of All Time," *Jezebel*, April 29, 2010, https://jezebel.com/dirty-dancing-is-the-greatest-movie-of-all-time-5527079.

In *Dirty Dancing*, Jewish identity is never spoken of directly but it's alluded to. It's a Jewish film, Bergstein told *Tablet Magazine*, "if you know what you're looking at."[12] Race is also never explicitly addressed, and even though Black music and Black and Latin dance are everywhere in the film and freedom riders are referenced, Black people barely exist in the world of Kellerman's. This partly stems from Bergstein's characterization of the summer of '63 — the last summer "you felt like you could reach out your hand and change the world" — and how it informs everything in the movie. It's one thing to be inspired by Black movements, as well as Black music, dance, and culture, as *Dirty Dancing* is; it's another to take from Black movements, music, dance, and culture without any real acknowledgement of Black innovators, artists, and leaders, while turning it all into fodder for the pleasure, edification, and "liberation" of white characters.

When Bergstein told the *New York Times* that she meant *Dirty Dancing* to be a celebration of the belief that "earnest, liberal action could remake the world in your own image" it's important to consider who the liberal is in that sentence. Remaking the world in the image of an affluent, thin, white, liberal, cisgender Jewish woman would be a wildly different world, but it's not an inclusive one. And we see that in the ways Black and Latinx culture is appropriated throughout the film without acknowledgment or any real engagement with those communities.

In her 2020 essay "Black Culture Without Black People," Imani Kai Johnson refers to appropriation as "colonialism at the

12 Aroesty.

scale of the dancing body or the sacred ritual object, its life and dynamism reduced to a thing for consumption or a costume for play."[13] Kai Johnson's essay centers hip-hop dance, but there are direct parallels to *Dirty Dancing*'s musical choices and choreography. Of the 12 songs on the film's official soundtrack, five are by Black musical artists and groups. In one iconic scene, Baby and Johnny playfully seduce each other to Mickey & Sylvia's call-and-answer duet, "Love Is Strange." They lip-sync, air guitar, and writhe their way through their own performance of this musical marvel without any acknowledgment of the Black artists whose voices they are literally embodying. I have loved this scene on many levels since the first time I saw *Dirty Dancing*, but it's impossible to ignore how it contributes to the film's appropriation of Black culture rather than any kind of appreciation. Latinx and Black forms of dance blend together to create the so-called "dirty dancing" that drives the film, but it's largely performed by white dancers throughout the movie, save for one nameless Black couple among the dancing staff in the worker's quarters, and Tito Suarez, the Black bandleader at Kellerman's, played by Black tap-dancing legend and actor Charles Coles.

"Black culture without Black people" is a deep flaw in *Dirty Dancing*'s foundation, and it seems to stem from Bergstein's real life outside of her screenplay. In a personal essay in 2008, Bergstein wrote that she was 14 when she discovered dirty dancing. "I first heard R&B on a radio in an alley; then I heard it

13 Imani Kai Johnson, "Black Culture Without Black People / Hip-Hop Dance Beyond Appropriation Discourse," in *Are You Entertained? Black Popular Culture in the Twenty-First Century* (Durham, NC: Duke University Press, 2020).

properly at a smoky basement dancing party, and I was gone. It was my rhythm. It was speaking to me! Dirty dancing came out of Brooklyn and Detroit, from an inner-city Black culture and an underground rhythm and blues. I found it ravishing."[14] Bergstein related to it, co-opted it, and eventually got very rich off of it, but in most of her interviews there's little acknowledgment of *Dirty Dancing*'s musical and choreographic origins in Black culture.

Bergstein is a progressive liberal who set out to make a deliberately and subversively progressive liberal film — which she did — but *Dirty Dancing* is also complicit in the long racist history of white people extracting from Black culture. In the closing of his essay, "White Enough," which appears in *The Time of Our Lives: Dirty Dancing and Popular Culture*, Richard Dyer writes, "Perhaps the persistence of *Dirty Dancing*'s nostalgia for a time of optimism, liberalism, and emerging sexual freedom is also a nostalgia for a time when all of that could still take place under the sign of whiteness."[15] It is necessary to grapple with this and make space for it alongside the ways in which the film more explicitly (and successfully) addresses other forms of inequality and discrimination.

In interviews, Bergstein talks a lot about the "upstairs/downstairs" division in *Dirty Dancing*, and the strata of class within those divisions but never about how race or gender intersect with class. At Kellerman's, there are four classes of workers:

---

14 "Best of Times, Worst of Times: Eleanor Bergstein," *Sunday Times*, September 21, 2008, https://www.thetimes.co.uk/article/best-of-times-worst-of-times-eleanor-bergstein-x9028vg22b0.

15 Richard Dyer, *The Time of Our Lives: Dirty Dancing and Popular Culture* (Wayne State University Press, 2013).

the manager and his nepo-baby nephew, the Ivy League waiters, the band leader Tito Suarez and the musicians, and finally the dancers entertaining the guests alongside the other physical laborers who clean up after them. The guests range from middle class (the Housemans) to upper middle class, with at least one set of criminals who present as upper middle class.

That first day at Kellerman's is when the audience witnesses Baby develop real-life class awareness. As she crosses over to Johnny and Penny's world, she sees the physical demands of their work and the hours of training that go into their artistry, but also the reality of precarious labor and abortion as health-care. As her knowledge of the world in the staff quarters grows, so too does her ability to perceive her father's assumptions about the character of working-class laborers. Baby is forced to see the barriers her father is complicit in upholding despite his talk of equality. "It's a film about community," Bergstein told Boston.com. "The subtext of the whole thing is that Johnny is a working-class boy. Baby, she thinks affirmative action is great but she doesn't understand 'union.'"[16]

Bergstein herself navigated these class boundaries (for example: choosing "dirty dancing" and Latin dance as opposed to a classical European or "higher" dance form like ballet) in her own life. And though she wanted to make a film with underlying

16 Meredith Goldstein, "Bringing 'Dirty Dancing' to Life: Eleanor Bergstein Infuses Stage Version With Political Punch Her Film Held Back," Boston.com, February 1, 2009, http://archive.boston.com/ae/theater_arts/articles/2009/02/01/bringing_dirty_dancing_to_life/.

sociopolitical themes, Bergstein is candid about the lengths she had to go to to get *Dirty Dancing* off the ground. It's a message film, she told Cleveland.com, but "God knows I didn't go around pitching it that way. I got up on tables and dirty danced for men in my short skirts — you did what you could to get this film made, so let's not make me grander than I am."[17] Bergstein implies that old-fashioned sexism was her biggest challenge in bringing her film to fruition. At first, no studio wanted to make *Dirty Dancing*. That title! Those dance moves! The abortion subplot! A lead character who's a teenage girl?! According to Bergstein, male executives loved the mixtape she sent along with the script, but they kept passing on making the actual movie.

Finally, MGM executive Eileen Miselle read the script and loved it. It was sexy, it had heart, and, most importantly, it was real. Before she was shuffled out of the company in a corporate regime change, Miselle helped Bergstein flesh out the script. Linda Gottlieb, another executive at MGM, stepped in and kept fighting for the film, ultimately serving as *Dirty Dancing*'s producer. But eventually MGM dropped its option on the script, and *Dirty Dancing* was desperately in need of a new home. Vestron, a video distributor that planned to get into the feature film business by making low-budget movies they could distribute directly, stepped up. They offered a modest budget, around five million dollars, and Bergstein and Gottlieb said yes.

Bergstein became a producer as well, and, as a result, was able to exert a level of ownership and control over *Dirty Dancing*

---

17 Simakis.

that few screenwriters ever know. She was able to ensure her script, her politics, and her creative vision guided everything from casting to filming to postproduction. Bergstein knew what music she wanted in every scene and had included 60 pages of dance instructions within the script. She and Gottlieb sought out filmmaker Emile Ardolino because they appreciated his Oscar-winning direction of Jacques d'Amboise's documentary, *He Makes Me Feel Like Dancin'*. Ardolino, above all else, understood how to shoot dance from the perspective of a dancer. He then hired choreographer Kenny Ortega, who was a protégé of Hollywood dance legend Gene Kelly.

After filming was over, Bergstein continued to hold her ground and fight for her film in the editing room. A big advertiser insisted the abortion subplot be scrapped, but Bergstein refused and would not back down (more on this in Chapter 4). When an editor suggested cutting a shot of a dance move that he thought was morally risqué, he was put in his place. It was based on Bergstein's own signature move: her leg up around her partner's neck. She told Yahoo, "At some point the editor said, 'I don't know if we should use this shot. I mean, how can you have respect for a girl who dances that way?' And there was this terrible silence, and people said, 'Well, actually, that's Eleanor's step.' So it was a little embarrassing."[18] I don't know if Bergstein means it was embarrassing for the film editor, everyone in the room, for her, or all of the aforementioned, but I'm personally embarrassed for the film editor who found himself scandalized by

---

18 Watkins.

a move like this in a film called *Dirty Dancing* and whose respect for women is so conditional he voiced his inane opinion when he could have just said nothing. I think about how exhausting it must have been for Bergstein to have to be ever-present at every creative step. I think about the labor she had to perform every damn day to ensure her vision made it onto the big screen intact.

The initial response to *Dirty Dancing* was uneven at best. After an advance private screening, one Hollywood exec advised Bergstein to burn the film and take the insurance money. According to Bergstein, everybody hated it — producers, exhibitors, and distributors. "They thought Jennifer was ugly, they thought Patrick was too old, they thought it was a stupid story, they didn't like the music."[19] But they screened the film for a general audience of moviegoers and the crowd went wild. When the film opened, audiences — and some critics — fell in love. Within a month, *Dirty Dancing* grossed more than quadruple its budget. The film, and its subsequent soundtrack, each topped their respective charts for months. By the time it became an Academy Award–winning film (winning best original song for "(I've Had) The Time of My Life"), *Dirty Dancing* was a bonafide hit.

---

19 Simakis.

2

Nobody Puts Baby in a Corner

BABY LOVE

Dirty Dancing was a hit and it helped make Patrick Swayze a star, but for me it was first and foremost about Baby. Right away I loved Frances Houseman. I didn't realize it then, but when she said "I carried a watermelon," I died alongside her and I continue to die every time I watch that painfully awkward and all-too-identifiable scene. Even at nine years old, I both *was* her and wanted to be her. I loved to read, I was considered smart, and I was deeply uncomfortable in my own body. I paid attention and noted everything, from the unspoken tells and meaningful glances between adults trying to have covert exchanges to overhearing conversations not meant for my ears when my teachers or parents were trying to sort out things they thought were above my head. One day I came home after meeting a friendly neighbor's husband for the first time and told my grandma the marriage wouldn't last, that he wasn't good enough for her. I was seven, but I was right. Within five years they'd divorced.

But the way that I was most like Baby was that I, too, wanted to change the world. As I moved into my early teens, I longed for Baby's slight evolution, her political and sexual awakening. I didn't want to change everything about myself; I trusted my own value to a certain extent. But having seen Baby's arc in *Dirty Dancing*, I hoped for a more emboldened version of myself tucked inside, ready to be revealed. A more confident, worldly, and embodied me could be montaged out if only the right circumstances conspired in my favor. I didn't need a metamorphosis or even a minor transformation, but I did want to come to a deeper understanding of myself and the real world.

At 17, Baby is a teen girl and the hero of *Dirty Dancing*. I wanted to be a teenaged hero. The combination of Bergstein's writing and Grey's nuanced performance offers a rare cinematic gift: a young woman who isn't perfect but who feels perfectly real and who gets to be the hero of her own story even though there's a big, strong man standing right beside her for most of the film. Baby drives the action, and the audience experiences the film almost exclusively from her point of view. Plus, Grey's performance as Baby is brilliant, and I continue to marvel to this day about the small choices she makes in every scene that create intimacy with the viewer and bring the audience closer to Baby with each screening.

As opposed to the majority of films which center the male gaze, a term coined in 1975 by feminist film critic Laura Mulvey,[20] Baby's gaze is given the priority, which continues to be something of a rarity even almost 40 years after *Dirty Dancing*'s debut. The camera lingers on Swayze's muscular, glistening body repeatedly, and he is typically the one wearing the least clothing throughout the film. Johnny is the object of Baby's sexual feelings and gaze. We're watching Baby and Johnny fall for each other, yes, but they do so over the course of building something else as well: a genuine partnership. Even through the film's final dance number, Baby's point of view as she is watching the staff dance from her position on the stage is centered and central to the collective liberation of Kellerman's.

LEADING WOMEN

Even though *Dirty Dancing* is definitely part romance, Bergstein makes plenty of space in her script for Baby's relationships with other women. I've always been especially fascinated by two of them: dance instructor Penny, and Baby's slightly older, more glamorous sister, Lisa.

Lisa and Penny are, at first glance, Baby's complete opposites. Like three different points on a triangle, Baby, Lisa, and

---

20 Rachael Sampson, "Film Theory 101 — Laura Mulvey: The Male Gaze Theory," *Film Inquiry*, October 27, 2015, https://www.filminquiry.com/film-theory-basics-laura-mulvey-male-gaze -theory/.

Penny seem to occupy their own corners of the world (and tropes of cinematic womanhood) with little overlap between them. Baby is studious, idealistic, and high-minded; Lisa is confident, vain, and seeking the spotlight; Penny is talented, dazzling, and "in trouble." All three have one common enemy, as it turns out: Robbie the creep. The Ivy League waiter asshole, a good-on-paper (he's going to be a doctor and comes from a "decent" family) misogynist who found his own reflection in Ayn Rand's *The Fountainhead* and is deeply irresponsible with his dick. Robbie is in his own triangle of opposites with Johnny and Dr. Houseman, but he has zero dimensionality. He's a privileged, sexist jerk with no attractive qualities beyond basic facial symmetry.

Like so many handsome, upper-working-class creeps, Robbie knows how to perform decency and impress up the social hierarchy to get what he wants, and this is where Penny's and Lisa's stories intersect. Upon the Housemans' arrival, Lisa and Robbie eye each other up almost immediately. After a few flirtatious encounters, Lisa asks Baby to cover for her so that she can rendezvous with Robbie on the golf course where there's a "nice view." The aftermath is anything but nice when Baby sees Lisa storm out of the bushes, clothes askew, and hears her angrily tell Robbie she "hasn't heard an apology yet." He tells her to go back to her mommy and daddy, maybe she'll hear one in her dreams. We the audience, and Baby and Lisa, know Robbie is a bad guy, but we don't yet understand how bad until Baby discovers Penny is pregnant and Robbie is the father. Penny's only option is an illegal abortion, which costs $250 — more money that Penny can even dream of.

When Baby hears this, she assumes that the matter will be easy to resolve: Robbie's got money, and he'll be accountable and give it to Penny. No problem. When confronted, Robbie denies paternity, essentially daring Penny to prove the fetus is his. He slut-shames her and theorizes that if she had sex with him, who knows how many other men she's also had. The double standards around women's sexual agency were ubiquitous and normalized in 1963 — and let's face it, in many ways they still are today. The disgusted, frustrated look on Penny's face at Baby's earnest belief in a tidy resolution conveys everything we need to know about the disparity between their realities. Penny can't deal with this kind of naivete when she's nursing her own anger and humiliation at believing Robbie loved her. "What's your name? Baby? You don't know shit about my problems . . . Go back to your playpen . . . *Baby*," Penny says, the force of her scorn almost throwing Baby out of the room.

Baby isn't deterred. She confronts Robbie the next morning, and when he smugly tells her that "some people count and some people don't," Baby glares at him and leans in to deliver her threat. She tells him to stay away from her sister or she'll have him fired. Then she dumps a jug of water all over his crotch. This moment is a satisfying early depiction of Baby's outrage at injustice and fearlessness when it comes to standing up to men, but it's also worth thinking about why she can lash out with confidence. In this situation, her class privilege protects her and she doesn't think twice about threatening Robbie's job. Penny, who has been on her own since she was 16, has never known that kind of entitlement. When Baby's face-off with Robbie doesn't go as planned, she has options. She asks her father for the money, and invokes his trust in her so he doesn't ask what the cash is for. Lying to her father's face that she won't use the funds for something illegal is her second rebellion of the day, and Baby's just getting started.

She brings the money to Penny and tells her to book the procedure. But there's a second snag: the "doctor" can only fit Penny in on the one night of the week when she and Johnny are to perform their infamous mambo routine at the Sheldrake Hotel. Penny is caught in an impossible situation — this pregnancy will ruin her life in every way, but the termination is just as ruinous in its own ways — and solidarity with Baby is the only option. Suddenly, Baby finds herself agreeing to undertake a crash course in mambo and fill in for Penny so that she can have the abortion and keep her job. Baby has not yet experienced the material and psychic burden of being precariously employed and at the mercy of exploitative working conditions. But Johnny and Penny are living it every day.

Watching Baby learn to dance under Johnny and Penny's tutelage is a wonderful study in eroticism, hard work, trust, and pleasure — for instructor and student — in both teaching and learning. When I was nine, the scene of Penny and Johnny dancing with Baby sandwiched between them seemed like a cool magic trick of synchronicity. By the time I was in my early teens, I was attuned to the sexual vibes emanating off their fully clothed, upright threesome. But there's also something that's just satisfying about watching these three people become bonded together in their shared goal of helping each other survive capitalism, misogyny, and the patriarchy through art. By the time we get to the Big Day, Penny and Baby have formed enough of a bond that Penny helps Baby get ready for the Sheldrake. When Baby forgets to take off her white cotton bra under the low-cut, sparkly mambo gown. Penny and Baby laugh but then Penny's face falls and her shoulders sink under her own anxiety and fear. Baby holds her new friend with tenderness, their roles reversing, Baby reassuring Penny that everything will be okay.

Because *Dirty Dancing* is aware of how women are denied sexual and reproductive agency, things are not okay for Penny. As Baby and Johnny celebrate their successful shows at the Sheldrake and begin to acknowledge their growing feelings for each other, they return to Kellerman's to discover the abortion doctor botched the procedure. Penny's in her cabin, crying in anguish from pain and possibly bleeding to death. Baby runs to get her father and silently retrieves his medical bag while she waits for him to get dressed. Dr. Houseman saves Penny, but his trust in Baby is broken. "Is this what my money paid for?" he asks Baby, anger and disappointment emanating from every inch of Jerry Orbach's body.

Baby's falling out with her father ripples into her relationship with Lisa, too. Lisa accuses Baby of just being upset that she's no longer Dr. Houseman's favorite, that her "Daddy's girl" bond has finally gone bust. But Lisa's triumph is short-lived.

When she makes her way to Robbie's cabin, she finds him in bed with Vivian Pressman (Miranda Garrison, a dancer and choreographer who pulled double duty as Ortega's assistant), the rich, bored housewife and noted "bungalow bunny" who buys "extra dance lessons" with Johnny anytime she wants. In her heartbreak, Lisa throws herself into Kellerman's annual end-of-summer talent show, the grand finale before everybody heads back to the city.

While Baby paints scenery, Lisa rehearses her culturally appropriative hula song and dance (during the actual show, she dons a coconut bra and grass skirt). The performance itself is so purposefully cringeworthy it borders on hilarious, an excellent indictment of what pretty, thin white girls can get away with as long as society agrees she's pretty. Lisa's movements are as stiff and stilted as her voice is off-tune. (Fun fact: Brucker reportedly wrote the hula song herself.) Baby has put in the time and deserves an opportunity to shine, while Lisa has thrown something together at the last minute that is just ghastly. The background/foreground of the sisters' dynamic is filmed here as they present to Kellerman's and to their family: Lisa in the spotlight, ungainly in her unearned confidence; Baby quietly off to the side painting background scenery when she, in fact, has genuine talent, skill, and experience performing onstage.

But above all they are sisters, and Bergstein's script affords them a tiny, almost throwaway scene that in a different movie would surely have been sacrificed for something with more momentum and less heart. It comes at a pivotal moment: Baby tearfully confronts her father and apologizes for disappointing him but doesn't let him off the hook for disappointing her in return. Afterward, Lisa sits next to her sister on the bed in their shared room and offers to do Baby's hair and make her pretty for the talent show. Then she catches herself and looks at Baby. "Never mind, it's prettier the way you wear it." The camera stays tight on their faces as Baby leans her head on Lisa's shoulder in a rare moment of closeness and gratitude.

I've always loved this scene so much, as well as the hug between Baby and Penny when they're getting ready for their respective big nights. Intimate moments of solidarity between women characters are rare in film, never mind in a summer romance dance musical movie. Baby and Penny's relationship is seeded in class conflict and opposition and ultimately blooms as an act of feminist care. Baby comes up with the money Penny needs for her abortion, but it's more than that: they spend hours and hours of rehearsal together as Penny mentors Baby, their bond deepening in the space of working towards a life-changing (and life-saving) shared goal. The relationship coalesces in that desperate hug that they both need, a tender moment of vulnerability as they arrive at the night they've both been working towards. When they meet again on the other side of their milestones, the outcomes couldn't be more different: Baby is basking in the glow of her triumph and Johnny's new-found appreciation, and Penny is hemorrhaging to death after a dangerous "dirty knife" abortion, or what was once referred to as a backroom or coat-hanger abortion. Baby jumps into action and doesn't think of the consequences she'll face for breaking the code of secrecy and for the lies she's told her parents. She wants to help save her friend's life and is willing to blow up her own to make that happen.

We don't get as many glimpses of Lisa and Baby's relationship as we do of Penny and Baby's, but I relate to the believable tension of their sisterhood (they're close in age but very different and cleaving to their own identity markers even if those exist only in opposition to each other, instead of independently of each other), the dramatically different ways they're forced to grow up during their time at Kellerman's, and where they finally find some commonality. From the film's first scene, we're shown and told that Lisa cares about "feminine" things like clothes, hair, makeup, and boys. Baby cares about injustice, economic equality, and the Peace Corps. Upon the family's arrival at Kellerman's, Lisa observes one bellhop struggling under the weight of a tall armful of shoeboxes that a guest has ostensibly packed for their vacation. Her regret is immediate and all-consuming. "I should have brought the coral shoes! You said I was taking too much!" Lisa tells her mother. Marjorie points out that Lisa packed ten pairs of shoes, but it doesn't matter. Dr. Houseman quickly jumps in and tells Lisa, "This is not a tragedy. A tragedy," he says, "are three men trapped in a mine, or police dogs used in Birmingham." His tone is teasing and affectionate, and definitely dismissive. Baby piles on, adding, "Monks burning themselves in protest." "Butt out, Baby," Lisa retorts. Later, in the dining hall, after Dr. Houseman explains that his youngest daughter's going to "change the world," Baby pipes up with a sneer to add that "Lisa's going to decorate it."

Later, Baby tries to impart some of her new woman-of-the-world wisdom to Lisa, telling her, essentially, that sex isn't just about doing it with a handsome Ivy League dirtbag who is going to be a doctor. "It's just wrong this way. It should be with someone . . . someone that you sort of love," Baby says. Lisa questions Baby's motivation. "Oh, come on. You don't care about me. You wouldn't care if I humped the entire army as long as they're on the right side of the Ho Chi Minh Trail. What you care about is that you're not Daddy's girl anymore. He listens when *I* talk now. And you hate that."

This dynamic between the sisters shows us that they've been raised to compete for their father's attention and have been conditioned as rivals thanks to a constant state of compare and contrast. The notion that both sisters contain multitudes is not recognized in the patriarchal structure of their familial hierarchy. It can only be achieved once the status quo has been upended and Baby's bravery/transgressions force the Houseman family to exist on a more even, honest, and equitable level rather than perched on pedestals that nobody can survive. In growing as individuals and encountering real-world challenges, Baby and Lisa are able to grow together, too.

THE "DIRTY" PART OF *DIRTY DANCING*

Sexual agency is an integral component of Baby's, Penny's, and Lisa's stories. In the beginning, Lisa and Penny are both initially fooled by Robbie's performance of being a catch: he looks clean cut, is handsome, and he's going to a fancy school to become a doctor. Penny thought that he really loved her, and Lisa finally gives in to his coercive tactics after rebuffing his advances on the golf course during their first date. Upon observing Baby and Johnny's closeness outside Johnny's cabin, Robbie makes disparaging comments about Baby and how he chose the wrong sister. Robbie has such low emotional intelligence that he can't recognize mutual attraction and genuine enthusiastic desire even when it's explicitly in his face. Robbie's last champion, Dr. Houseman, finally sees Robbie for the cowardly predator that he is when he hands Robbie an envelope of cash and wishes him good luck in medical school and Robbie in turn thanks him for all the help with "the Penny business." Dr. Houseman yanks back the cash in disgust.

Comparatively, Baby's sexual relationship with Johnny can be read as a portrayal of the feminist ideal of agency. She's a college-bound young woman who is of the age of consent in New York State, and her journey in *Dirty Dancing* is one towards body autonomy and expressing sexual desire. Baby knows what she wants, she knows what this relationship is, and she's under no illusions — she is always in the moment, and unlike Lisa's out-loud musings about her and Robbie's potential tenth wedding anniversary, Baby is not looking towards an imagined future as Mrs. Johnny Castle.

She and Johnny have had an intense crash course in trust building and intimacy, spending hours and hours learning to move in sync with each other, respond to each other's bodies, find each other's rhythms; they do literal trust falls in a lake over and over and over as they practice the dreaded lift. Once the big dance is over, the adrenaline and endorphins and hormones have no place to go. Add to that a scary confrontation with mortality via Penny in medical crisis, and the fallout with Baby's relationship with Dr. Houseman, and it's a complex mix of motivations and emotions that leads Baby to Johnny's door in the middle of the night.

Baby's main goal, let's be clear, is to shoot her shot. Baby wants to have sex with Johnny and their intimate scene is a study in non-verbal enthusiastic consent.

Baby is not ashamed of her sexual needs. In most other films that depict the terrible aftermath of an illegal abortion, the message is almost always that sex is bad (or sex is bad when it's performed by certain women) and comes with terrible consequences, i.e., nearly dying as a punishment for premarital sex. *Dirty Dancing* does not fuck with this harmful trope. Penny is never judged for having sex (not by anyone that matters, at least), or for her pregnancy, or for getting the abortion. Where other films would make her a cautionary tale or portray her as "asking for it," Penny is cared for by her community and valued and supported by them. *Dirty Dancing* refuses to moralize sex as bad. Sex with Robbie is bad because he is bad. Sex in and of itself is not bad. Baby wants to have sex and there's fallout from that, but not because she has sex. Instead, she has to weather the unfair consequences from refusing to be devalued as a person just because she's defied her father's expectations. In the world of *Dirty Dancing*, young women have sexual agency. These are its two great, enduring gifts: the normalization of abortion as necessary, life-saving healthcare, and the normalization of women wanting and having sex.

Before Baby and Johnny have sex, however, they up the stakes dramatically by articulating what they mean to each other. Baby is mortified by how her father behaves towards Johnny in the aftermath of saving Penny's life. She shows up at Johnny's partly to apologize for her father and Johnny, shirtless and still shaken by the evening's events, downplays it. He could never save Penny like Dr. Houseman. "That's something. The reason people treat me like I'm nothing is because I am nothing," Johnny says. Baby counters, "That's not true! You — you're everything!" But Johnny won't or can't hear the subtext of Baby's accidental confession, the excruciating level of earnestness in her words. They argue about scarcity and hope, each of them reciting their own limitations and also reappraising each other. It's the end of one part of their relationship and the beginning of something new, something more.

Johnny says he's never met anybody like Baby, fearless and idealistic and brave. Baby says she is scared of one thing: leaving Kellerman's and never feeling again in her whole life the way she feels when she's with Johnny. Hearts on sleeves, Baby asks Johnny to dance with her. "Here?" he asks. "Here," she says, and crosses the room, closing the short distance between them. She lightly caresses his gleaming, muscled chest and Johnny's body shudders with a sigh that holds the weight of this moment, the eroticism of her touch, and the relief of someone like Baby seeing his worth. Their bodies practically melt together, and the electricity between Jennifer Grey and

Patrick Swayze almost sets the screen on fire. Their hands travel each other's bodies with an urgent hunger, but they take their time with each other, too. They breathe each other in, stare into each other's eyes, and Baby kisses Johnny's neck as he throws his head back. She walks around his back, lightly kissing his shoulders and then cupping his left butt cheek with her hand before coming back to the front of his body. He holds her and lifts her arms up to pull her simple white shirt over her head. They kiss, finally, and keep dancing until they cut briefly to the pair in bed.

The power dynamics of Baby and Johnny's romance play out the next day during a postcoital pillow talk. Johnny asks about Baby's real name, and after she tells him he calls her Frances. There are a few ways of thinking about this: Johnny would simply like to know the given name of his new bed guest. He's falling for Baby and wants to know everything he can about her as their relationship grows. Johnny also hears the "ick" factor every time he has to say "Baby" to this young woman he has just had sex with. And it's also just a very obvious acknowledgment of Baby's post-virginity transition to womanhood and the reclamation of her real name, Frances.

In this moment, Baby must figure out how to navigate her new worldliness. She asks Johnny how many women he's "had." Johnny is uncomfortable and his class-based insecurities come tumbling out as he reflects on the women — rich, beautiful, and they "smell so good" — who throw themselves at him. These women feel entitled to buy his body and his services, seeing him as a sex object or a commodity rather than a real person. They use him, he tells Baby, not the other way around. The implied sex work aspect further complicates the power dynamic between Baby and Johnny. He is hired help, working poor, and desperate to keep this job that both exploits him and also artificially inflates his ego. Baby is a resort guest, the privileged daughter of Mr. Kellerman's doctor friend, and explicitly off-limits to a man like Johnny. He might be expected to make himself "available" to the older, bored, rich wives, but Mr. Kellerman strictly forbids Johnny to engage in any way with the daughters beyond teaching them to dance. The younger generation are reserved for the Ivy League waiters, like Robbie, whom Mr. Kellerman has specifically hired and recruited. These young men are meant to show "the goddamn daughters a good time . . . Schlepp them out to the terrace, show 'em the stars. Romance 'em any way you want."

Ultimately though, the age difference between Baby and Johnny is the most obvious indicator of inequity between them. Baby is likely about 17 and Grey passes as such, while Johnny is supposed to be about 24 years old. Swayze looks incredible in *Dirty Dancing*, but he does not pull off 24 — *maybe* 26 or 27. In reality, Swayze was 34 during filming and Grey was 26. But at 17, every year older matters, because that life experience is still factoring into our developing brains. What dials down the squick factor, for me at least, in Baby and Johnny's romance is that Baby is the legal age of consent, and she's also in full understanding of what this relationship is. She has total agency, maybe for the first time in her life, and she's making decisions that feel good to her and for her. There is nothing coercive or duplicitous about Johnny, nor anything dangerous. In fact, he's a deeply loyal friend and caring partner — and Baby witnesses that firsthand in the dynamic between Johnny and Penny. Baby initiates every single aspect of her relationship with Johnny, and he appreciates her toughness, intelligence, work ethic, and idealism. His sexual attraction to Baby comes *after* they've spent a lot of time together and he's fallen for her personality. The age difference between the two is just one aspect of the multilayered imbalances that complicate Baby and Johnny's romance. The fact that she's legally able to consent to their relationship, and that we see her do so enthusiastically, helps put distance between the audience and social "ick" factor of the years separating the characters and the actors.

A HERO NAMED BABY

That Johnny falls for Baby as a person first is another part of *Dirty Dancing* that I've always loved. Jennifer Grey was and is beautiful, but she didn't present like many other Hollywood-type ingenues of the period who standardized a certain look: blond, blue eyed, thin with boobs, pouty mouth, button nose. Bergstein has gone on the record stating that industry execs said it wasn't believable that Johnny would fall for Baby when Penny was right there. There was a distinct anti-Semitic thread in the ongoing conversation about Grey's "attractiveness," and in her memoir, Grey herself talks at length about her complicated lifelong relationship with her nose being big and therefore reading "too Jewish."

Bergstein was adamant that Grey's look was exactly what she envisioned for Baby. It's easy to look back on the film now, with the understanding of how much Bergstein's own story informed aspects of *Dirty Dancing* and conclude that Bergstein wanted to see a version of herself represented onscreen that was not available to her as a teen. Bergstein's radical belief in her vision is how *Dirty Dancing* actually got made, of course, and it's worth identifying what she was fighting for: that stories of teenage girls, and in Baby's case, Jewish teenage girls, deserved to be told; that Baby, and by extension Bergstein, deserved to be the hero of her own story and get the guy; and that dance, music, sex, classism, justice, and abortion rights were inextricably connected because that's how it was in real life, too.

At first, even Swayze didn't fully buy that Johnny would fall for Baby when he had a woman who looked like Penny as his dance partner. He eventually wrapped his head around it by arriving at this conclusion: "It's [*Dirty Dancing*] got so much heart, to me. It's not about the sensuality; it's really about people trying to find themselves, this young dance instructor feeling like he's nothing but a product, and this young girl trying to find out who she is in a society of restrictions when she has such an amazing take on things. On a certain level, it's really about the fabulous, funky little Jewish girl getting the guy because [of] what she's got in her heart."[21] He wasn't

21 Tiffany Green, "Dirty Dancing: Behind-The-Scenes of an 80s Movie Classic," *Collider*, March 17, 2019, https://collider.com/galleries/dirty-dancing-behind-the-scenes/.

completely wrong, of course, Baby is fabulous and funky. But to deny that Grey had what would easily be considered a "perfect" body, and was attractive and compelling in her own regard, is to be complicit in supporting an exclusionary standard of beauty that upholds anti-Semitism.

At nine years old, I didn't have any awareness of the anti-Semitism fueling some of the critiques of Grey's appearance, but I remember being thrilled by the singularity of her look. She had curly hair and small eyes, like me, and even though she was thin and I was fat, I recognized the awkwardness in her body before Baby eventually learns to dance and gains more confidence.

As Baby, Grey represented another kind of beauty and another kind of sexy, both of which were vitally important to me as a fat kid. There was almost nobody who looked like me on screens big or small that wasn't being ridiculed, hated, or mocked. Fat girls and women weren't going to get the guy, they weren't going to fight to make the world a better place, and they weren't going to learn to dance. Fat girls only cared about getting thin or going on diets or hating their bodies. Fat girls were best friends and sidekicks (Natalie on *The Facts of Life*) or caretakers (Nell on *Gimme a Break!*) at best, and objects of disdain, cruelty, jokes, and/or pranks at worst. Fat girls didn't exist except in relation to thinness: desperately working towards it, failing at it, or being too morally flawed to achieve it. Fat girls didn't have discipline or good hygiene (the number of people who believe this to this day astounds me!), didn't care about themselves or their bodies, must be depressed or disturbed or lazy or greedy or some combination thereof. Fat girls were rendered invisible, except for when people wanted to point out that we were taking up too much space or too many resources. Fat girls had few options, so I read myself in characters to whom I related best, the ones I wanted to be like in some form.

Our bodies didn't look the same, that was fine, but Grey as Baby brought "unconventional," "non-standardized" beauty and sexuality into my pop culture consciousness. Beyond her appearance, Baby was also a quiet rebel and burgeoning feminist interested in exploring her own pleasure, confronting her own privilege, subverting expectations, challenging the status quo, and demanding accountability from the men in her life — she was the hero I needed. Baby tries to do the right thing over and over. Even when the right thing is the hard thing, she steps up, a trait she demonstrates consistently throughout *Dirty Dancing*. When Johnny is wrongfully accused of stealing from the resort's guests, Baby identifies who the real thieves are and publicly lays out her case against them. When that doesn't work, she confesses that she also knows Johnny couldn't have stolen the goods because she was with him. All night. This admission, in 1963, is explosive. Baby has openly admitted to having sex with Johnny, crossing class boundaries, defying her father, and, in so doing, she exposes the seedy behind-the-scenes drama of what transpires between Kellerman's guests and the hired help.

Later, Johnny finds Baby in his room. He's been looking all over for her: Baby was right when she named the elderly

Shoemacher couple as the real thieves. They're wanted all over the East Coast. But Johnny is still fired; his affair with Baby means he's out. Baby is bitter and devastated, and rails about the injustice of it all and that her confession was for nothing. But Johnny doesn't see it that way. He can't believe she stood up for him; her faith in him and her belief in doing the right thing renew his belief in himself and the world. He loads his belongings into his car, they hug and kiss and say goodbye, and Johnny drives away a changed man, revving the engine to kick up a cloud of dust behind him, literally obscuring himself from Baby's sight. Baby has changed, too. It's a rainy afternoon and Dr. Houseman is sitting on a covered patio lost in thought, angry and mournful that this family trip had a daughter deflowering package that he did not sign up for.

"You're not who I thought you were, Baby," he tells his daughter. Baby tearfully accepts this as true, but she also has some things to say. She tells him she's sorry she disappointed him, but that he's disappointed her, too. He always told her everybody deserves equal treatment, but she sees that he really meant everybody like them, not people like Johnny. When Baby says, "I let you down, Daddy. But you let me down, too," it's devastating. Grey's heartbreaking vulnerability as she weeps is affecting enough, but when Jerry Orbach's eyes fill with tears at the stinging truth of his daughter's words, well, I am a mess every time.

As someone who was extremely close to my father, this scene always stood out to me. My dad died when I was 17, the age Baby is in *Dirty Dancing*. Up to that point, we'd only had a few instances of friction that stemmed from who I was becoming and whether it was at odds with his expectations of me. I know he wanted me to go to college or university, and I know he was irritated that I wasn't willing to share my writing with him, aside from the pieces that were already published.

We were working class and definitely more on the side of working poor. Eventually, the biggest conflict between my father and me became my desire for upward mobility. I wanted some amalgamation of the lives I'd been reading about and watching on screens my whole life. I wanted to work as a writer, I wanted to talk about highbrow and lowbrow pop culture, and I wanted to go to a university that would take me away from the tiny confines of the two-bedroom apartment that my grandma, dad, sister, and I called home. My dad had already transcended the intense poverty and scarcity of his own upbringing, as well as the unpredictability and violence of my alcoholic grandfather. Dad, who left home at 14, had become a business owner and worked for himself and we were often hand-to-mouth, but we still had enough that he prioritized taking care of other people. He was smart, but he wasn't educated, something that he deeply wanted for his children. But when he envisioned our lives further into the future, he most wanted a kind of enmeshment that gave me a slight ache in my stomach and my heart.

I had begun to feel a little trapped that his vision of the future wasn't as big as mine. I didn't even know how to articulate my biggest dreams. But he had already articulated his: that we would all own a house together one day. Home ownership for all of us was the ultimate goal for my dad, something he had wanted for himself but especially for his children, who he had raised to feel safe and loved. He couldn't ever imagine that we wouldn't want to remain in a secure and stable family home, something he had never had himself. But he had already provided that for me, even if it was a small apartment, which is why I was able to want something of my own.

My father died before we could ever have this confrontation or any resolution. I will always be devastated by this loss and I still miss him. I often read us into fictional father-daughter stories and play out how the same conversations and scenarios might have transpired between us. Baby idolized her father, and in turn, Dr. Houseman took pride in their shared values, but they are not carbon copies. The moment where Baby holds herself and her father accountable is a huge turning point in the growth of these two characters, and in the trajectory of their future relationship. Baby realizes her dad is a complex person with flaws. Dr. Houseman hears Baby call him in and then he must also accept that she is similarly a complex person with flaws. This scene is what makes *Dirty Dancing*'s big dance finale even more triumphant. Baby has already done the truly hard work in standing up for herself, standing up to her father, and standing up for justice.

When Johnny strides back into Kellerman's and decides that he won't be chased off, that he will leave on his own terms, we know that his bravery has been inspired by Baby and her belief in him. He walks with confidence over to the Housemans' table and utters the famous line "Nobody puts Baby in a corner" and holds out his hand, inviting Baby to join him. Together they walk up onstage, interrupting the end-of-season finale, and claim the spotlight. Johnny apologizes for the disruption but asserts that he always performs the last dance and tonight will not be any different. His partner will be, though. He introduces Frances Houseman to the room.

The music begins and Dr. Houseman moves to get out of his chair until Marjorie Houseman tells him to sit back down. As they watch Baby and Johnny dance, Marjorie is beaming with pride and visibly thrilled. "I think she gets it from me!" she proclaims. When the dance reaches the moment leading up to the lift, Johnny checks in with Baby silently from across the room. She nods, runs towards him and . . . they nail it. The real-life celebration on set bleeds into what we see onscreen as well: Grey had yet to actually nail the lift with Swayze until the time came to film it. Baby's reluctance mirrored Grey's, so the radiance on both Baby's and Johnny's faces was absolutely informed by the actors' own emotions at clearing this last, major filming hurdle. Baby has conquered her fears and, when the room explodes into dance around her, she's also helped revolutionize Kellerman's, at least for one night. As Baby dances, the camera pans to the other women in Baby's life: Marjorie is joyfully dancing up a storm with Dr. Houseman; Penny is grooving with Tito, the band leader; and Billy, Johnny's cousin, is trying to teach a happy, eager Lisa how to loosen up her hips.

Dirty Dancing is a love story, but it's not just Baby and Johnny's love story. There's love between Baby and Penny, and between Baby and Lisa. It's also Baby's love story with herself. And *Dirty Dancing* is screenwriter Eleanor Bergstein's love story with dance, with her life, and with writing strong, nuanced, complicated women characters into being.

This feminist-centered creativity has frustrated, infuriated, and confused many men her entire professional career. I think about how hard Bergstein worked to get *Dirty Dancing* made, and that for the most part only women executives saw its potential and value. I think about the men who liked the music but didn't think much of a movie with a teenaged girl protagonist, or who thought Grey wasn't attractive enough to be the lead, or who encouraged Bergstein to burn the negative and collect the insurance money. I also think about that 1973 *New York Times* review of Bergstein's novel by Anatole Broyard — how the story of its two main characters, both women, is essentially a waste of his time — and Elisa Gonzales's feminist unpacking of his critique almost 50 years later in the *Paris Review*. Broyard expresses his exhaustion at the whiplash flashes of Bergstein's talent, and exasperation that she hasn't written the story of these two female protagonists the way he thinks she should have. "Why in the world are you doing that, Ms. Bergstein?" he writes.[22] Gonzales quotes him and responds, "I think I know: the search for a passionate connection with life is chaotic; the lives of young women encompass more than a man thinks they should."

Making space for the actual complexity of our living, from the sprawling mess, wondrous chaos, and quiet stillness, to the

---

22 Broyard.

constellations of grief, volcanic rage, and defiant, deliberate, delicious joy, this is actually the central thesis of Bergstein's work, and what I've spent my whole life responding to and working towards.

Baby, Lisa, and Penny didn't necessarily reflect my reality, but I relate to aspects of all of them. I think of the fragments of feminist relatability I've collected over the years — Baby, Miss Piggy, Clair Huxtable, Claudia Kishi, Ursula, and Murphy Brown to name a few — and how they've informed the development of my personality and core beliefs. And it's not just the fictional women characters that helped shape me, but the women writers, actors, and artists who fought to make these characters so vivid and vital. Bergstein and Baby are critical contributors to my pop-culture DNA and also to who I am as a person. And Bergstein even deserves partial credit for my career as a music journalist and how I've used music as a lens through which to explore feminism, equity, justice, social issues, and culture. *Dirty Dancing* changed my life, and a big part of that is how the *Dirty Dancing* soundtrack introduced me to a whole other way of listening to music, engaging with its rhythms and pulses across eras and decades, and diving into a song's moods and hues. Even now, after more than a decade writing about music, I'm still trying to make sense of the blockbuster success of the *Dirty Dancing* soundtrack and how it became one of the bestselling albums of all time.

3

From Mixtape to Bestselling Soundtrack: The Music That Makes *Dirty Dancing*

HEY! BABY

When I was very little, the Mini Pops made some of my favorite music. The concept is simple if a little creepy in hindsight: really young children perform covers of popular songs by grown-ups. This led to relatively innocent fare like an even sunnier version of the Monkees' "Daydream Believer" to more complicated to adapt choices like "Bette Davis Eyes." The song selections spanned genres and decades, almost defiantly, but each compilation was actually a pretty clever blend of hit songs and targeted demographic. It was kid-friendly music because kids were singing the songs, but the children were singing songs beloved by their parents and grandparents and caregivers, basically anybody 20 to 50 years old at least.

My favorite Mini Pops record was also the biggest Mini Pops record in Canada and was briefly the third-highest-selling record in the country: 1983's *We're the Mini Pops* was released on both vinyl and cassette, and our house had copies in both formats. My sister and I were obsessed. Revisiting the tracklist now, I understand why: "Fame," "Eye of the Tiger," "Kids in America," "Mickey," "I Love Rock 'n' Roll," "Satisfaction," "Don't You Want Me," "Bette Davis Eyes," the Mini Motown Medley featuring "ABC," "Baby Love," "Dancing in the Street," "My Cherie Amour," and "Sugar, Sugar." Now arguably some of those songs might not have been ideal content for my four-year-old self, but I was already watching *The Muppet Show* and *The Young and the Restless*. I'd seen some stuff.

The Mini Pops were my gateway to a seemingly jumbled and juxtaposed overview of mid- to late-20th-century soul, R&B, rock, and pop. The Mini Pops laid the foundation, but the *Dirty Dancing* soundtrack became one of the building blocks of my love of music and making meaning out of mixtapes. On the surface, the *Dirty Dancing* soundtrack doesn't make any sense. It ebbs and flows between upbeat '80s pop and rock that would find a permanent place on adult contemporary radio stations and '60s pop, soul, and rock 'n' roll hits with a few hidden gems just offbeat enough to evoke a timeless kind of vintage nostalgia. Well before the movie got made, it was screenwriter and producer Bergstein's *Dirty Dancing* mixtape that hooked people long enough to get them to even take a look at the script before eventually rejecting it.

I love the almost mythmaking level of detail Bergstein says she dove into not only while writing the script, but during the painstaking descriptions of how the dancing should look at every turn. But before she did any of that, she started with the music. I am delighted by the image of Bergstein playing living-room DJ for her family and friends, keeping track of which of her favorite songs from the '50s and '60s launched everyone onto their feet and into dance-party mode. I'm thrilled by the anachronistic mix of songs spilling across four decades, the sonic terrain shifting genres and moods, keeping the audience in a state of heightened curiosity as we try to anticipate and locate ourselves in the competing timelines of the film's setting, the year in which it was released, and whenever we're watching it in the present day.

The contemporary songs on the *Dirty Dancing* soundtrack are big and polished, even bombastic in the case of Alfie Zappacosta's "Overload," but they are mostly blunt declarations in the pursuit of romance and/or sex. They are songs in that they meet the criteria of being contained units of lyrics and music, but that's the extent of their measurability, reflecting the slick-but-unsubtle Wall Street–influenced 1980s. It was all plastic, nothing organic, and the shine stayed surface level. Many of the vintage songs can't help but stand out in contrast as being fundamentally more interesting, authentic, creative, and occasionally iconic because of the context in which they were created.

Consider "Be My Baby," which was recorded by the Ronettes in 1963, and is widely considered to be one of the most important and best songs in the history of rock 'n' roll. The Ronettes were a young girl group signed to Phil Spector's Phillies label, but Ronnie Bennett was the sole Ronette to actually appear on the song. She was just 18 years old at the time, one year older than Baby, when she recorded the track. Spector was already a famous and famously volatile music producer and songwriter about to revolutionize pop and rock music with his signature "Wall of Sound" style. "Be My Baby" was the first song to feature the ambitious, dense, and intricately arranged and engineered production style, and the layers of instrumentation parallel the complexity of what was happening in the recording studio. Spector, who was married at the time, fell for Ronnie Bennett, and she was soon under his spell, too. Like Baby and Johnny, Bennett and Spector's affair began in 1963, and Spector was five years Bennett's senior and her boss. But that was the extent of the parallels between them. Their relationship took a dark turn and their eventual marriage and subsequent divorce became the subject of Ronnie Spector's 1990 memoir, *Be My Baby: How I Survived Mascara, Miniskirts, and Madness, Or, My Life as a Fabulous Ronette*.

The intolerable violence of the Spector marriage is a complicated aspect of the song's legacy, but in a 2013 interview with the *New York Times*, Ronnie Spector recalled the innocence at the heart of "Be My Baby" as part of its sustained power. "I was so much in love. That energy comes back to me every time: when I'm singing 'Be My Baby,' I'm thinking of us in the studio."[23]

"Be My Baby" is the crowning glory of a much-hyped playlist. With *Dirty Dancing*, the music was the only thing everybody was enthusiastic about from the beginning. A 1987 interview with the *New York Times* would help substantiate *Dirty Dancing* as a film of actual merit, and in it, Bergstein broke down her song curation process: "The selections fall into three basic camps: fairly tame Latin music for the Kellerman's dance floor; 'clean teen' pop (Frankie Valli's 'Big Girls Don't Cry') for the Houseman cabin; and sensual rock and soul (Otis Redding's 'Love Man,' the Contours' 'Do You Love Me') for the staff quarters. These last songs speak directly to Baby Houseman from 'the physical world.'" Bergstein explained: "I tried to choose the harshest music I could find, the music that would be most sexually shocking to a young woman who'd never heard it before. Because I imagine that in Baby's bedroom at home there'd be early Joan Baez, the Weavers, maybe Harry Belafonte."[24]

Once *Dirty Dancing* was finally greenlit, securing the rights to the songs Bergstein wanted was as crucial as the correct casting. But music rights cost a lot of money, and the crew was working with a modest budget for a feature film of under $5 million. In the *Dirty Dancing* episode of *The Movies That Made Us*, which details a lot of the struggles that went on behind

23 Marc Spitz, "Still Tingling Spines, 50 Years Later," *New York Times*, August 16, 2013, https://www.nytimes.com/2013/08/18/movies/be-my-baby-a-hit-single-with-staying-power.html.

24 Freedman.

the scenes, Bergstein elaborates, "Music is the soundtrack of the heart and I couldn't picture lines of dialogue without the songs."[25] Co-producer Linda Gottlieb acknowledged that whatever she had in the budget, she knew they'd need it for the music, but it was a process that took longer than any of them imagined. Choreographer Kenny Ortega and assistant choreographer Miranda Garrison (who also played married bungalow bunny Vivian Pressman) had to resort to choreographing to music that wasn't going to be in the movie, after the first person they hired to obtain the music rights got nowhere and was fired.

Patrick Swayze pitched his own song, one that he'd co-written for a movie a few years earlier that ultimately wasn't used. Gottlieb loved "She's Like the Wind" so they had that to work with, but it wasn't used in a scene that required choreography. Finally they brought a man named Jimmy Ienner on board, whose tactics proved successful immediately. "He claimed he went down on Phil Spector's big toe," Bergstein says in *The Movies That Made Us*. "He kept saying, 'The girl has to have it,' and he came back with the rights to 'Be My Baby.'"[26] According to Gottlieb, "We paid more for that song than any song in the movie, and I think it lasts 45 seconds. My recollection is it was something like $75,000, which was beyond comprehension for a film with a total budget of $4.5 million. But it was so worth it."[27]

25 *The Movies That Made Us*, episode 1, "Dirty Dancing," directed by Brian Volk-Weiss, aired November 29, 2019, on Netflix.

26 *The Movies That Made Us*.

27 Spitz.

In the end, Ienner secured the rights to all of the songs that Bergstein wanted. But, there was still another major piece of music missing: an anthem worthy of ringing in one iconic last dance.

SOUNDTRACKING THE LIFT

Truth be told, I like Bill Medley just fine, but I never much cared whether it was him singing "(I've Had) The Time of My Life" or some other golden-throated dude. I love Jennifer Warnes, though; frankly, I think Medley's voice takes up too much space. It's a lopsided balance incongruous with *Dirty Dancing*. I wouldn't be surprised if Medley watched the film and thought Johnny Castle was the main character. That's the energy he's bringing to the song; if he really understood the assignment, he'd have been more of a supporting figure to Warnes in the finished recording. According to an interview with *Rolling Stone*, Medley didn't even want to take on the song when he was first pitched, and he wasn't the first to say no. Donna Summer and Lionel Richie passed, and so did Daryl Hall and Kim Carnes. Medley thought *Dirty Dancing* sounded like the name of a bad porn and he didn't want to leave his pregnant wife, who was due any day, at home in California while he went to write and record the song in New York. Medley said no and kept saying no until Ienner wore him down with calls and flattery, and (most importantly) confirmed that Warnes was in.

It wasn't a guarantee that the song would be what Ortega and the team would ultimately choose for the big finale. In *The Movies That Made Us*, Ortega talks about rehearsing without any music and combing through tape after tape with Miranda Garrison. When they finally worked their way to the last cassette, Medley's voice filled their ears, followed by Warnes's warm alto, then the beat dropped and the tempo kicked up. A slow tease, a buildup, and then fireworks. "That's the song!" Ortega remembers saying. They played it non-stop for three days while Grey, Swayze, and the entire cast rehearsed and filmed take after take.[28]

With that final scene in the can, the team started working on a rough cut that they could show to hotshot Hollywood producer Aaron Russo. Afterward, Russo turned to the *Dirty Dancing* team and told them to burn the negative and collect the insurance and then he walked out.

In the *Dirty Dancing* episode of *The Movies that Made Us*, Mitchell Cannold, Vestron's senior VP of production, admits he was "terrified" Vestron higher-ups would just trash the film. The hope had been that *Dirty Dancing* would get at least a week-long theatrical release and then Vestron would send *Dirty Dancing* straight to video, which was, after all, the company's specialty. But then the fledgling studio decided to do a test screening of the film for one thousand people. At the end of the movie, the crowd went wild and Vestron committed to a full theatrical release, not just a week-long run. *Dirty Dancing*

28 *The Movies That Made Us*.

opened on August 21, 1987, and even though there were plenty of negative reviews (including from Roger Ebert, who gave the film one star), there were also some positive ones. More importantly, audience word of mouth, the original viral marketing, spread across North America and around the world. People loved *Dirty Dancing*, and they loved its soundtrack, too.

#1 AT THE BOX OFFICE AND ON THE BILLBOARD CHARTS

The film spent 19 weeks at the top of the box office; *Dirty Dancing*, the major motion picture soundtrack, spent 18 weeks at the top of the Billboard charts. "(I've Had) The Time of My Life" was number one all over the world, and "She's Like the Wind," "Hungry Eyes," and "Yes" charted as well. It revitalized musical careers that had stalled two decades earlier and launched a surprising but familiar face as a new singer-songwriter. *Rolling Stone* called it the last of the blockbuster albums, and as of this writing, it's sold more than 32 million copies. But the soundtrack's overwhelming success (it sold an estimated seven million copies in its first year alone) meant that executives wanted to cash in, while also wanting to give the fans what they wanted. In March 1988, a second soundtrack was released, *More Dirty Dancing*, and later that year, a *Dirty Dancing* concert tour took the show on the road with Bill Medley, Merry Clayton, the Contours, Eric Carmen, and several dancers. Vestron turned this concert tour into a concert film, and there's a full bootleg on YouTube that is worth checking out, if only to marvel at what a blatant cash grab/ fan service it was. Like *Dirty Dancing*, the concert film opens with a classic girl-group number (the Shirelles' "Will You Love Me Tomorrow") and a shot of young people dancing (this time the choreographed dancers in the live concert). But rather than matching any of the urgency or coy teasing of the film's title sequence, the song is slower and mournful, raising questions that Baby and Johnny never asked. The dancers are spread out and spaced far apart on the stage and the video editor slows down their moves, sapping the urgency out of their bodies and libidos. It's like a parody of an ad for a diet version of a delicious food: the same name as *Dirty Dancing*, none of the flavor.

Dirty Dancing's song selection collapsed space and time, creating a kind of anachronistic jukebox hodgepodge that should have been hot nonsense but was instead somehow wildly enthralling and tonally perfect for millions of fans across generations. I will not pretend to adore every single song on the original soundtrack; some songs mean more to me because of how they're used in the movie versus standing alone on their own merit. What follows is my definitive ranking of the 12 songs of the original *Dirty Dancing* soundtrack.

1. "Be My Baby," The Ronettes

If this isn't your favorite track, well then, I don't know how to help you. From the hollow kick of the bass drum and the shimmer of cymbals to the percussive roll of the castanets and the lush layers of strings, piano, and brass, the musical arrangement is flawless. Ronnie Spector is one of the greatest voices of all time, and there's a deeply compelling edge to her performance here. She's flirting but she's also matter-of-fact in what she wants; it's an early anthem for aspiring feminists who like making the first move (which applies to both Baby and me). She even snaps a couple of her words, sweetly coy bordering on brash, and there's a hint of impatience tucked inside her tone that adds tension to the lush, romantic, doo-wop backdrop. In a 2013 *New York Times* retrospective of the song's importance, Marc Spitz writes that the song is "as much about power and control as it is about romance. Lyrically it also marks a bold moment in pop music, when a woman makes a play for a man while infantilizing him. Usually the reverse was the norm."[29] Spector was also a Black woman in 1963 singing about her desire, expressing an agency that wasn't typical of the time in pop music. Spector pours herself into the song — it's unmistakably her voice at its center — and the context of the recording needs to be acknowledged, especially when it's used to soundtrack the coming of age of a young white woman in a film that uses Black art, dance, and culture but has almost no Black people in it. In *Shine Bright: A Very Personal History of Black Women in Pop*, Danyel Smith writes about the lengthy history of pop music and its roots in Black music, vocal styles, dance, and culture. White artists and producers stole from Black artists whose contributions were then (and continue to

29 Spitz.

be) ignored, overlooked, and deliberately erased. *Dirty Dancing* perpetuates this appropriation.

Thanks to the song's iconic nature and ubiquity — as of 2013, it was estimated that the song had been featured 3.9 million times on radio and television[30] — "Be My Baby" is also the perfect entry point for a film like *Dirty Dancing* that plays fast and loose with the time-space continuum. The song is both disorienting to a contemporary audience, yet so familiar and beloved that it's comforting. Its inherent allure is amplified by the sexiness of the film's opening credits and the flashes of thighs and legs of couples dirty dancing all over the screen. We're voyeurs all together in this moment, and these credits, paired with this song, play up the promise of the film's title, even if the film itself delivers an infinitely more chaste experience.

2. "Love Is Strange," Mickey & Sylvia

I may never have heard this song were it not for *Dirty Dancing*, and for that alone I'm forever grateful to Bergstein. But even more so? The absolutely charming, sexy cringe of the scene in which the song is used is one of my all-time favorite dance sequences in the movie. Baby and Johnny have danced their big mambo number at the Sheldrake, they've had sex, and now this dance time in the studio is extended public foreplay. It's

---

30 Spitz.

also a brilliant bit of script-flipping as Baby repeats back to Johnny all the dance rules he barked at her in the beginning of their rehearsals. She is feeling herself, and her confidence shines as she takes the lead. The more Johnny chases Baby, the more she plays hard to get with a joking sternness that he must respect her space. It's teasing, sexy, and goofy — a metaphorical dance within their literal one — and then they level up their play with an actual lip sync to this aptly titled song. It is both devastatingly embarrassing and sexy and it took me years until I truly understood just how ridiculous and silly two people can be when they're in the first throes of mutual attraction. It's heady and hot, but it's also dorky and makes you behave in ways that you'd otherwise consider totally humiliating if you had to witness them between other people. Love is strange, it's a fact, and this song and scene capture it perfectly.

3. "Hey! Baby," Bruce Channel

Yes, songs with the word "baby" in the title are a little obvious for this movie, but this one is so fun and upbeat, and it also features incredible harmonica work. It is a fantastic framing for the infamous log scene, where Johnny and Baby try to work on Baby's stability and core strength. The decision to keep the cameras rolling during a lot of the dance rehearsals captured some key moments that helped connect Grey and Swayze's offscreen dynamic to Baby and Johnny's. Grey's scared, trilling laugh as she teeters on the log feels extremely real, but the song's relentless cheerfulness ensures we're in on the giddy excitement of what's transpiring between the two. It's also a key part of witnessing Baby's determination in action: over and over we see her do things that scare her, intimidate her, and over and over we see her fail and over and over we see her try again.

4. "Stay," Maurice Williams and the Zodiacs

The lyrics of this song foreshadow one aspect of the film (Baby defying Dr. Houseman) as Williams croons to the object of his affection that her parents won't mind if she has another dance, she should stay a little longer. The doo-wop shuffle and the sexy timber of Williams's warm bedroom voice are the perfect vehicles to convince a girl to break curfew and keep kicking it late into the night. In the movie, the song is playing when Baby returns to the crowded dance floor from the night before. She makes her way through the dimly lit room, searches each pair, and finds Penny and Johnny wrapped in each other's arms, swaying back and forth. As Maurice Williams's falsetto soars, Baby reveals that she has the money Penny needs for her abortion. But the release in the chorus and the relief on Penny's face are both temporary. There are more complications to come, just like in the song; even though Williams promises things will be fine if the object of his affection stays, he can't actually guarantee that. Baby has come up with the cash, but that's just one solution to a multipart problem. Someone needs to learn Penny's mambo routine and fill in for her with Johnny or they risk losing an important and financially critical gig at the Sheldrake and the lives they've built for themselves. "Stay" is a song about risking it all for an act of rebellion, which is exactly what Baby does.

5. "In the Still of the Night," The Five Satins

This song is classic doo-wop — a tender, romantic number that's pure nostalgia and full of promise. Listening to it, you can feel a glowing full moon, stardust shuffling across the sky, and the deep velour quiet that only 3 a.m. can bring. There's a luminous resonance to the saxophone solo that breaks me in half in the best way every time I hear it. It's the perfect song for Johnny's confession to Baby that he dreams of her father's acceptance, and she tenderly holds him as they spend the night together. *Dirty Dancing* has so much to say about what makes a "good man," and over and over we see Johnny model all the ways in which he rejects and refuses toxic masculinity. His vulnerabilities and insecurities are eye-opening to Baby; by virtue of her privileges, she is utterly sure of herself in ways that he'll never be. Johnny has street smarts and a cynical worldliness that Baby may never have, but she has a hope and belief in the world that fuels her resilience. This is their last night together, the summer is over, and they have helped each other change and grow into better versions of themselves because they've shared their vulnerabilities and truths. This song captures the profound beauty of finding someone else who will hold you and see you in the ways you have always longed for.

This is the first version of "You Don't Own Me" that I ever heard. I didn't know Leslie Gore's version existed until I was a teenager at the very least, and I knew nothing about the Blow Monkeys, but even from my first listen to this song, I was drawn to the come-hither swing and swagger as well as the singer's voice and the way that the words almost slithered from their mouth. There was something mysterious and sly about the singer's performance, and the words dripped with a defiance I gravitated towards. The whole thing felt subversive and transgressive, and I liked not knowing if the voice singing to me was a man or a woman, but rather something more than those narrow labels. Dr. Robert, the lead singer, is a man and I really appreciate that he doesn't waste his time on fragile masculinity or feel compelled to change the lyrics. The song also embraces the time/space/genre collapse of the whole album, with elements of doo-wop, torchsinger cabaret, '80s synth pop, and new wave. The song's placement in the movie is subtle but purposeful: Baby and Johnny have their first fight as a "couple" — she accuses him of not standing up for himself and he must remind her, again, that he needs this job. Then Baby sees her father with Lisa and Robbie and grabs Johnny's arm, forcing them to crouch down out of sight. Johnny bitterly points out that Baby literally isn't standing up for him with her father. "You Don't Own Me" slinks in as Baby searches for Johnny to apologize for her hypocrisy.

Throughout *Dirty Dancing*, we see Baby's ideals clash in real life, and that "real life" looks different for different people due to class privilege. In Leslie Gore's original, the listener hears "You Don't Own Me" as a definitive rejection of the patriarchal concept of women as property of men. In the Blow Monkeys' cover, the vocal plays with gender conformity and queerness, a willful interrogation that moves the song beyond the binary and asks us to consider a multiplicity of power dynamics. Johnny is owned by Kellerman's. He's found himself literally up for sale to the bungalow bunnies, and by virtue of his station in life — he's working poor, he comes from "nothing" — he feels like he's nothing. He has big dance dreams but a job with the local painter's union is the only thing waiting for him back home; his options are limited. Baby is only now realizing that inequality exists all around her, and that she's part of it. Baby is from a Jewish family and born directly after the end of World War II. She grew up with the Holocaust as a recent memory, which makes her aware of and sensitive to injustice. But like all of us, she, as a young person, learns that privilege is relational and situational. Like Baby, I was once a young woman who thought she had some understanding of marginalization and otherness because of my gender, growing up on the poor end of working class, and my fat body. But I only really understood *my* perspective, and I had to learn that intersecting factors and hierarchies of race, gender, sexuality, and other things all contribute to how people treat others. Baby, in *Dirty Dancing*, has to learn to understand class, as uncomfortable as that might make her and her father.

Bouncing and bopping with the same kind of triumphant, climactic utterance of its actual title, Merry Clayton deserved a better song than this for her big moment in the spotlight, but she sings the hell out of it. From romance novels to pornographic films, "Yes!" is the classic imagined feminine cry of satisfaction, but the song itself is weirdly conservative if you think about its context. This woman is finally ready to lose her virginity because she's in love, and she imagines a night of euphemisms like squeezing and hugging and kissing, but it's also unabashedly a celebration of "making love" and all of the sex that the protagonist will finally have with her man. Clayton's performance is what elevates the song far above its lyrics, and the song's placement in the movie helps create a masterful moment of high tragicomedy.

The song soundtracks Lisa's high-heeled walk to Robbie's cabin. She wears a beautiful dress and her bravado is tangible as she practices her smile, but so are her nerves (she takes a deep breath to steel herself as she approaches the door). The viewer knows that Robbie is a jerk, and yes, Baby attempts to talk her out of it, but she doesn't go so far as to tell her sister just how bad this guy is. Baby also doesn't mention that she saw Lisa and Robbie storm off the golf course a few weeks earlier, that she saw Lisa flustered, upset, trying to rearrange her mussed-up clothes, and asking for an apology. That kind of fraught non-consensual experience was normalized for a lot of young women in 1963, and it's a stark contrast to the enthusiastic consent between Baby and Johnny. Lisa is caught up in the fantasy of perfection — she's already fantasizing about their possible return to Kellerman's for their tenth wedding anniversary — and has decided she's ready to "go all the way" with Robbie. It's clear from Lisa's expectant smile that she genuinely believes she's going to bestow something momentous upon him, but she's also anxious. She steels herself, ignores the sock on his door knob, and bursts into the cabin. Lisa's smile drops immediately as she sees Vivian Pressman riding her boyfriend. Lisa's naivete is shattered, but she has further irrefutable proof of the real Robbie. "Yes," indeed.

8. "(I've Had) The Time of My Life," Bill Medley and Jennifer Warnes

The Academy Award–winning song is epic and euphoric and appropriately celebratory of something that burns bright and fast. It is past tense, just like Baby and Johnny will be once they both depart Kellerman's the next day, but there are no regrets here. It's all just gratitude and triumph, affection and lust, a shared acknowledgment that this unforgettable experience has changed them both. It's profound and exhilarating that Baby and Johnny never talk about forever, or even talk about being in love. It feels especially radical considering the societal norm in 1963 that sex and marriage went hand in hand. It speaks to Baby's burgeoning feminism and her activist spirit that she wants to subvert the status quo, and it also speaks to how she listens to her own body. Baby wants pleasure and she's not ashamed of it.

I always thought the feminist ideal of romance would be an almost ESP-like clarity between partners about the reality of what a relationship is: is it just sex, is it casual, is it something more, is there honesty and transparency, is it just playing games or even a competition? Baby and Johnny's intuitive relationship is a healthy pop culture ideal that I added to the fictional relationships I was most drawn to as a kid, like Miss Piggy and Kermit or Sam and Diane. These are couples with tension who are still drawn to each other, who would answer the will they or won't they in the affirmative, even if it doesn't stay that way. Baby and Johnny start off in conflict and one-sided attraction (Baby's) and their relationship morphs in the way I'd dreamed of. They care about each other, but there aren't any declarations, not really, other than a mutual admission that they have no regrets. There is a public, unspoken declaration of what they mean to each other, and that's the last dance.

When Johnny storms into the room, he's standing up for himself and for Baby. When he says, "Nobody puts Baby in a corner," he's not liberating her, he's affirming what she has already made clear to her family and to everyone at Kellerman's. They see her now in the fullness of who she is; they're about to understand her in a way they never imagined. When Baby and Johnny dance to "(I've Had) The Time of My Life" it is a euphoric celebration of an end that was always mutually understood. Bergstein's script lets the dancing and the music convey the depth of their feelings, and Grey and Swayze's chemistry conveys the attraction between their characters. Forever is a promise, but it can also lead to a crushing codependency, bitterness, loneliness, or some combination thereof. There's a freedom to seeing the fleeting not as failure but as temporarily transcendent, and this song and movie are perfect vehicles for that messaging.

9. "She's Like the Wind," Patrick Swayze

My least favorite kind of a love song is the one in which the male singer puts the woman subject onto a pedestal so high she's not even human anymore; she's a deified savior and shiny object of desire. But ultimately, every damn time, she's a source of validation for the man singing her "praises." The politics of the patriarchy and heteronormative relationships are alive and well in Swayze's song, which he co-wrote, but so is his vulnerability, as well as his devotion to his wife, Lisa Niemi, who is said to be the inspiration for the song. This was one of the big singles from the soundtrack in 1987, and one of the things that stands up so well decades later is just how super '80s it sounds. Saxophone and keys and electric guitar swirl and whirl, a stormy sea of anguish and desire that complements Swayze's brand of soft, earnest machismo just perfectly.

10. "Hungry Eyes," Eric Carmen

Carmen's predatory lyrics are a significant departure from "She's Like the Wind," but the very specific use of the song in *Dirty Dancing* make it a much steamier, sexier affair than it ever deserved to be. The song soundtracks one of the best "learning to do something" montages in movie history. It starts with Johnny teaching Baby to not only hear his heartbeat, but feel the rhythm of it, too. It then shifts to Johnny and Penny and Baby in the studio together, and shifts again to Baby sandwiched between the two experts, all three moving in sync. Even though their bodies aren't touching, there's an erotic charge at this unexpected threesome moving as one. It's also a thrill to watch them practicing their craft and seeing Baby master something so difficult. The song plays out as the sequence cuts between different rehearsal moments, interweaving the progress of the real dancing with funny, relatable accidents taken from actual rehearsal footage. Baby spins back too hard and knocks heads with Johnny. Johnny attempts to run his hand down Baby's side, a sexy, self-serious moment that sends Baby collapsing into giggles again and again as he inadvertently tickles her armpit. Grey was learning to dance in real time under Swayze and Rhodes's tutelage, and the choice to let that bleed into Baby's evolution is genius. The close-ups on the actors' barely clothed bodies don't hurt, either.

11. "Overload," Alfie Zappacosta

Some of the songs came cheap, and this is one of those tracks. The heavy synths, guitars, horn, and driving drums flex like they're keeping the beat while Zappacosta is benching weights at the gym. If you really listen to the lyrics, "Overload" sounds like a euphemism for blue balls, and like the singer/protagonist is desperate for release. That the song follows "Hungry Eyes" in the film, just after Baby has lost it on Johnny and yells at him for being impatient, is clever placement but it doesn't do much to elevate the actual song. When Johnny decides that a change of scenery will help get them back on track, the song provides the right momentum as they burn rubber and blow off some steam, and in that way it works.

12. "Where Are You Tonight?" Tom Johnston

It starts off as an upbeat shrug of a tune and features a few high points, but otherwise "Where Are You Tonight?" is unexceptional and inoffensive. It does feature great backup singers and excellent brass flourishes, and it successfully collapses space and time with major '50s-meets-'80s vibes. But without its placement in this movie and on this soundtrack, it's ultimately pretty forgettable. I wish with my whole heart that Solomon Burke's "Cry to Me" or Otis Redding's "Love Man" (both featured on *More Dirty Dancing*) had found places on the original soundtrack. They are better songs than this, and more deserving of the attention that has been heaped upon this album.

One song that is not on the soundtrack, understandably, is the Kellerman's Farewell, performed at the end of the talent show on the last night, an end-of-season show swan song annual tradition. The song moves in and out of foreground and background. It's a long number and I can't imagine sitting through it every year as a returning guest, but it serves a great purpose leading up to the iconic final dance sequence. During the number, Tito and Mr. Kellerman have a brief and kind of jarring conversation about what they and Kellerman's have survived so far. Then Kellerman laments that "it" feels like it's ending, that something is over. Kids, he says, don't want to come do the foxtrot with their family anymore. They want to travel to Europe and see 21 countries in three days. Exaggerative itinerary aside, Kellerman's fear is obsolescence more specifically but also that the world is getting bigger, which to him means his piece of it is getting smaller. It's an understandable concern, especially for an older Jewish man who has survived World War II. But there's also something else going on. It's no accident that Mr. Kellerman appears on stage just as the song reaches the crucial line, "But the heart needs a vacation, where no cares are seen." There's something ominous and prescient about this lyric, and I like to imagine a young Mike White watching *Dirty Dancing* over and over, this throwaway song lyric seeping into his subconscious, seeding the concept for *The White Lotus* more than 35 years later.

Kellerman's aims to be picture perfect and family-friendly, but there's rot underneath: class-based hierarchies; Ivy League waiters told to seduce young, rich women; racism, sexism, and so much more. But there's also the potential to challenge the status quo and revolutionize the whole place. Kellerman's represents both the '60s belief in the possibility of fundamental systemic change and the '50s and '80s impulses to pretend everything isn't just fine, it's great, actually. The Kellerman's farewell song sings of one thing but signifies another; it's a fascinating bit of original music in a movie soundtrack filled with songs that lived previous cultural lives before becoming part of *Dirty Dancing* history.

For many *Dirty Dancing* fans, the music and the dancing are inextricably tied together, and that was always Bergstein's intention from the beginning. The partnership of music and dance is why the film is so beloved, and why it has endured generation to generation. *Dirty Dancing* expanded my relationship to music, and also helped me think more deeply about the songs that permeate pop culture. Music is rarely ever just apolitical entertainment, because we bring ourselves — and the politics inherent to our identities and communities — to the listening experience while musicians bring themselves and their experiences into their art. Music is a portal through which we can relate to other people's truths, cultures, and experiences. Music can be a vehicle for joy and power, liberation and movement, creating change and subverting the status quo, as Baby tries to do throughout the film. Music is the soundtrack to the dance of life, as someone like Bergstein might say, and it's corny and cliché but it's true. Baby is going through an accelerated emotional and political evolution in *Dirty Dancing*, and the music keeps time, punctuating every milestone, every dismantled barrier, and every new adult emotion she feels. Music is also, for me, a lens through which I write about feminism and social issues, such as discrimination and resistance, equity and justice, as I imagine an older, wiser Baby might have done ten years in her future. This was one of my earliest takeaways from *Dirty Dancing*: radical acts can happen anywhere. Even in a summer romance dance musical movie whose plot is driven by one woman's unwanted pregnancy and her quest for an abortion.

4

The Case for Safe Abortions:
A Subplot of Substance

DIRTY DANCING IS AN ABORTION MOVIE

Dirty Dancing is an abortion movie. Yes, "dirty" and "dancing" are in the title, and dance is the medium through which our leads fall in love and ultimately find their own liberation, but it's the pressing need for an abortion that drives the action. When the abortion is botched and the woman almost dies — all because abortion is criminalized and not legally recognized as essential healthcare — the same group of people rally around the woman again to ensure she's seen by a credible medical doctor and to care for her as she convalesces. Community care as feminist practice is one of *Dirty Dancing*'s enduring lessons and (unfortunately still) radical statements.

When it comes to reproductive rights, *Dirty Dancing* is also something of a time capsule in the worst possible way. Set in 1963, *Dirty Dancing* depicts a time when abortion is illegal and illustrates quite clearly that this is an act of violence towards women, particularly poor working women. The movie was released in 1987 when abortion was legal in America and had been for 14 years, since the Supreme Court upheld Roe v. Wade in 1973. Even then, Bergstein was concerned about Roe v. Wade being overturned. She was adamant that the abortion subplot was integral to *Dirty Dancing*, and it would be deliberately worded and appropriately harsh, reflecting the reality of what it was like pre-1973, before people with unwanted pregnancies had legal access to terminate pregnancies safely. She was politically engaged and she remembered very well what it was like before Roe v. Wade became law — and she feared what would happen if (and, as it turns out, when) it was overturned.

We don't see the abortion itself onscreen, but we do experience its aftermath in deliberately horrifying and accurate detail. It's juxtaposed with a major achievement, something that would have been the climactic scene in many other films. After the physically demanding and rigorous hours of rehearsal, Johnny and Baby successfully nail their mambo performances (minus the lift) at the Sheldrake and experience a major high driving home from the gig. They're extra exhilarated that they weren't spotted by the elderly couple from Kellerman's who walked in mid-set, and Johnny becomes even more excited when he sneaks a glance at Baby changing outfits in the backseat of the car. They laugh and bond and rehash their successful night, giddy and aware of the vibe growing between them. Back at Kellerman's they hold hands as they leave Johnny's car, but the euphoria is swiftly upended. Penny is gravely ill.

The procedure was violent and awful, and we hear it described in horrific detail by Billy, who accompanied Penny to the appointment. There were "dirty knives" and no hospital bed, just a folding table, and the "doctor" didn't give Penny anything for pain. They locked the door and Billy could only hear Penny screaming and screaming and he tried to break the door down. We see Penny in bed, sweaty, septic, and writhing in pain. When Dr. Houseman arrives, he takes swift control of the situation, soothing Penny and asking who is responsible for her. Johnny says he is, and Dr. Houseman can barely hide his anger and disgust. Cut to Johnny, Baby, and Billy waiting outside Penny's room, everybody anxious for Dr. Houseman's prognosis. When he finally emerges, Penny is out of danger but everything has changed. *Dirty Dancing* has changed.

From song selection to the 60 pages of detailed dance instructions, Bergstein was purposeful in every word of the script, and that included the botched procedure. "I left the abortion in [*Dirty Dancing*] through a lot of pushback from everybody, and when it came time to shoot it, I made it very clear that we would leave in what is, for me, very purple language . . . I had a doctor on set to make sure [the description of the illegal abortion] was right," Bergstein explained in an interview with *Broadly*. "The reason I put that language in there was because I felt that — even with it being a coat-hanger abortion — a whole generation of young people, and women especially . . . wouldn't understand what [the illegal abortion] was. So I put very, very graphic language in, and I worked very hard on shooting it to make sure it was shown realistically."[31]

She knew what she needed to do to ensure that the messaging — abortion is essential healthcare — reached far beyond already pro-choice audiences. "You can make a [serious] film, and only people who agree with you will see it," Bergstein told *Forward*. Or, "You can make a film about true love and wonderful music and pretty dancing and sexy people, and have in it a lovely girl who ends up with a dirty knife and a folding table screaming in the hallway, and maybe you understand it."[32]

Bergstein felt that the best chance to really influence young people about the pre-Roe realities was to tuck it into a mainstream movie with sexy music, dance, and people. She wasn't sure exactly how deeply successful the message was in reaching *Dirty Dancing*'s audience over the years, until 2010, when a *Jezebel* writer called Bergstein for an interview. The screenwriter was surprised that all the interviewer's questions were about *Dirty Dancing*'s political themes.

"She said I should go online and look at the [comments], so I did and of course there were hundreds and hundreds of young women saying that they realized this movie was not a guilty

31 Marisa Crawford, "The Back-Alley Abortion That Almost Didn't Make It into 'Dirty Dancing,'" *VICE*, August 21, 2017, https://www.vice.com/en/article/433a99/the-back-alley -abortion-that-almost-didnt-make-it-into-dirty-dancing.

32 Irene Katz Connelly, "Will the New 'Dirty Dancing' Live up to the Original's Brave Look at Abortion?" *Forward*, August 17, 2020, https://forward.com/culture/452596/new-dirty-dancing -jennifer-grey-original-abortion-plot-pro-choice/.

pleasure, that so many of their moral and political attitudes came from it, so that was lovely. Then there was a cartoon in *The New Yorker* that had a man at a rally saying to a woman, 'What is a coat-hanger abortion?' And she says, 'Haven't you seen *Dirty Dancing*?' That was a big, big sea change in everything."[33]

DIRTY DANCING RADICALIZED ME

Add my voice to the countless online comments, editorials, and blog entries and interviews by and about young feminists across generations: *Dirty Dancing* is the first time I ever saw an abortion depicted onscreen. I didn't really understand what was happening to Penny on first viewing, but I knew it was important. Every time I rewatched the movie — we're talking probably hundreds of times before I was 20 — I was struck by Baby's desire to help Penny. Sure, she thinks there are easy answers and fixes to every problem, but that's not the worst quality to have. It helped reinforce a belief that I could do anything, too. Injustice in our high school's career preparation program? I could write an editorial about it that would be so provocative the program would come under review! (That same editorial helped get the paper banned, so it also backfired, but it confirmed a lot of my growing beliefs about oppressive forces, censorship, and the fragility of adults in the face of righteous teens.)

---

33 Crawford.

It took me longer to grasp the full financial, physical, and emotional burden of criminalized abortion on Penny and anyone like her who couldn't afford to pay for a private, discreet, and safe under-the-table procedure, people who were forced to rely on "back alley" providers and dangerous at-home, DIY terminations. By my early teens, I was a passionate advocate for choice and normalizing abortion in pop culture, the media, and in conversations with friends. I remember long, late-night discussions with a high-school best friend after we graduated. She was visiting me during my summer internship in New York City (I was working for *Soap Opera Weekly*), and one night we lay in the dark arguing for hours. She had been raised religiously, and though she'd drifted from her childhood church in her teens, in a few years she would join a new-to-her church to walk hand in hand with Jesus. (I'm paraphrasing but that was the literal visual she offered.) She confessed that she wasn't sure she supported a woman's right to choose and I lost my goddamn mind. We were 20-year-old feminists in the summer of 1999; bodily autonomy was our ongoing fight to carry on.

My own radicalization was furthered by the Vancouver chapter of Rock for Choice, an annual benefit concert inspired by the original co-founded in 1991 by feminist rock band L7 and *LA Weekly* music critic Sue Cummings. The first show in Los Angeles featured Nirvana, Hole, L7, and Sister Double Happiness and raised money for pro-choice movements working to keep abortion, abortion providers, and people seeking abortions safe from a series of bombing attacks by fundamentalist anti-choice protesters. The official Rock for Choice benefits ran from 1991 to 2001. Vancouver held its first Rock for Choice in 1994 and continued holding them annually until at least 2005. I love Rock for Choice and felt deeply empowered by the activists and organizers who set up tables offering up everything from homemade mixtapes, buttons, and stickers to riot grrrl–inspired zines and pamphlets about knowing our bodies and our rights. I remember the shock I felt when I heard about ostensibly liberal and progressive companies that donated to anti-choice politicians. The cry that echoed around the room when one of the organizers revealed a cherished sandal company had contributed to anti-choice causes was unlike any collective gasp I'd ever heard, and I had attended Take Back the Night rallies. The betrayal was palpable.

LOSE THE ABORTION, LOSE THE MOVIE

A corporate sponsor of the film (an acne treatment aimed at teens) also attempted to censor *Dirty Dancing* before its release, but Bergstein had a card up her sleeve. She was so committed to depicting the reality of a pre-Roe America, she made abortion integral to the whole plot of *Dirty Dancing*. If anybody tried to censor the film and cut the abortion, the whole reason for the movie would cease to exist.

> The studio came to me and said, "Okay, Eleanor, we'll pay for you to go back into the editing room and take the abortion out." And I had always known this day

would come — and that I could then say, "Honestly, I would be happy to, but if I take it out, the whole story collapses. There's no reason for Baby to help Penny, for her to dance or fall in love with Johnny. None of these things will happen without the abortion, so I simply can't do it even though I'd be so happy to do what you want." So we lost our national sponsor. What I always say to people — since people are always complaining that they put serious moral themes in their movies that get taken out — is that if you're putting in a political theme, you really better have it written into the story, because otherwise the day will come when they'll tell you to take it out. And if they can, it will go out. If it's in the corner of the frame, it will always go out.[34]

Edit out the abortion and Baby never has to fill in for Penny, Baby and Johnny aren't forced to spend hours upon hours rehearsing and dancing, the intensity of the situation isn't heightened by the impossible timeframe of the task at hand, there is no mounting sexual tension between them, and no real risk to Penny's and Johnny's livelihoods. Without the abortion, Baby never asks her father for money or lies to him about what it's for; she never unleashes her inner dancer, or falls for Johnny, or stands up for him in front of her whole family and Kellerman's when he's wrongly accused of a crime. Sans the

34 Crawford.

abortion, Baby never confronts her father's hypocrisy, tearfully telling him that both of their feelings matter equally. Without the abortion, Baby would never have been able to dance her truth in the big finale, nail the lift, and affirm that just because she loves to dance "like that" doesn't mean she isn't someone who wants to change the world.

I reached a new depth in my personal appreciation for *Dirty Dancing*'s abortion subplot when I was in my early 20s and a friend asked me to accompany her to terminate her pregnancy. I said yes immediately. On the morning of her appointment, she got into my car a little apprehensive and scared. She had zero doubts or regrets, but she wasn't sure what to expect when we arrived at the clinic. Would there be zealot-like protesters with misspelled graphic signs using religious iconography, gross photos, emotional manipulation, and violence to deter people from entering and accessing their medical procedures? She didn't do silence well, so we joked and found things to laugh and talk about as I drove. I was only present with one part of my brain because I was concentrating on the road and I was mentally preparing to shield her physically if some unhinged anti-choice freak turned violent. I'd never really been in a physical fight with a stranger before, though, and secretly I knew I'd probably be useless. My friend was way more likely to punch an aggressor and save us both. But ten minutes later we arrived, nothing between us and the non-descript doors other than a semi-crowded parking lot. We went inside and checked my friend in, then they whisked her inside another set of doors and directed me to the waiting room. I don't remember how long she was gone, but when they came to bring me in so that I could sit with her in recovery, I wasn't sure what to expect. Rows of gurneys and incoherent patients in various combinations of exhaustion, trauma, regret, and thankfulness?

Instead it was a crowded room full of mostly young women sitting in blue hospital nightgowns in muted moss green pleather chairs. Most seemed fine, quiet and relieved, some were talking to their companions, love and support emanated all around. Some of the patients made conversation with each other, forming fast bonds in the landscape of after. It was one of the most feminist spaces I've ever experienced, and I've always wanted to write a short story or a play that at least starts in the post-procedure room of an abortion clinic. It wasn't a radical utopia; there was a wide range of experiences evident throughout the room. A few people seemed fully checked out as if they'd already disassociated from the entire experience. Some people were alone and seemed happier for it, some people were accompanied by folks who looked like they'd rather be anywhere but this room full of "consequences." I didn't get their disapproval or their judgmental vibes. Abortion had been around forever. How could there still be so much stigma? Especially here, in a seemingly progressive and left-leaning city like Vancouver?

As a smug Canadian living in British Columbia, I grew up thinking that I had always had access to safe, legal abortions. I was wrong. Medically necessary abortions within nine weeks of conception were legalized in 1969, but there had to be proof that it was a therapeutic procedure that would save the child-bearer's life. All other abortions remained criminal-ized until 1988 when the Supreme Court of Canada struck down the 1969 act as unconstitutional and a violation of the Canadian Charter of Rights and Freedoms' guarantee of every individual's "life, liberty and security of the person." The U.S. Supreme Court had legalized abortion in 1973, a full 15 years before it was fully legalized in Canada. I was shocked. I thought abortion had just been legal in Canada my whole life.

Throughout my 20s and 30s, I watched other countries around the world fight to legalize, decriminalize, and nor-malize abortion as healthcare. I cheered the activists on as they made progress around the world. I knew it was vital to destig-matize abortion and talk about it openly and honestly. I knew we had to keep showing up in the streets and with our votes in support of choice and abortion as healthcare. Yet I see now that even though I grew up with *Dirty Dancing*, I still took abortion for granted. When terrorists attacked abortion providers and clinics, I was horrified but reassured myself that this type of extremism was extraordinarily rare and not reflective of the actual politics of most lawmakers, or, honestly, most voters. I was mostly unconcerned by what I believed to be the minority anti-choice opposition. A disparate group that I imagined was comprised of terrorists, rich white Conservative women, other religious zealots, science-deniers, misogynists, and far-right political hypocrites. Could this wild mishmash of people effectively mobilize to overturn Roe v. Wade? No way. I also naively believed that the Supreme Court was legally obligated to maintaining a separation between church and state despite the fact that so many American laws are fundamentally tied to biblical texts.

In some ways, I am still as idealistic and naive as 17-year-old Baby. I didn't think the world and reproductive rights could slide so far backwards. Even in 2017, following the election of the most willfully ignorant, openly ill-informed, misogynistic, callous, death cult capitalist of all time, I had hoped that the swing towards the far right would be temporary. It was particularly galling to watch a total and utter failure (in business, television, and humanity) pretend to be Christian (in the same way that many far-right people misuse Christian values to justify hateful rhetoric and actions) and activate hordes of fawning racist, sexist, homophobic, hypocritical, hateful bullies. I had never thought of myself as painfully naive or ignorant, but I am a white, cisgender woman and I was stunned and sickened.

On June 24, 2022, after 52 years of access to safe, legal abortions, an increasingly right-wing and evangelical U.S. Supreme Court overturned Roe v. Wade and let individual states decide whether people with uteruses still had the right to choose what to do with their bodies and how to live in them. It wasn't until Joe Biden's administration that the Supreme Court overturned Roe v. Wade, but it was Donald Trump's legacy after he had appointed and confirmed an accused sexual predator to the bench. Suddenly, *Dirty Dancing* had gone from containing a subtle cautionary look-how-far-we've-come tale about pre-Roe America to existing in a very different hellscape: post-Roe America.

Post-Roe America has dealt a series of devastating blows to pregnant people seeking safe abortions. Several states now have total abortion bans, which give fetuses more rights than the fully formed people carrying those fetuses. It is a wildly twisted interpretation of the American dream to privilege the potential of life over actual living, breathing human beings. People are charged and jailed for going out of state to have abortions, are denied birth control, and refused medical treatment. IVF doctors have been threatened with criminal charges if they discard unused embryos, leaving patients in limbo.

A month before Roe v. Wade was overturned, *Slate* published an article urging everyone to remember *Dirty Dancing*'s abortion story, zeroing in on the cost of the procedure in 1963 and the sheer impossibility of the amount for someone like Penny versus someone like Baby. *Slate* calculated that $250 would be roughly equal to $2,300 in 2022 and confirmed in an interview with Bergstein that she had personally researched the cost of obtaining an illegal abortion in the area of Kellerman's in New Paltz, New York. It would be an outrageous amount for the young working dancers, Bergstein said, estimating that even if they all pooled their wages they wouldn't be able to swing that amount because they were working for room, board, and tips.

Even where possible, getting a legal abortion costs money, something Bergstein admitted she hadn't considered until a few years ago when she participated in a fundraiser screening and Q&A.

I didn't understand until I had that Q&A afterwards that this was to raise money for people who couldn't scrape together the money even for a *legal* abortion, that it was still sometimes you had to go to another county or you had to even get to another state if it were past a certain month or something. That was an eye-opener for me. If you don't have money, everything is hard — I mean, it's hard to keep food on the table, it's hard to have milk for your baby, everything is hard. But I hadn't really spent a lot of time thinking of how hard it was to get a legal abortion.[35]

Even Bergstein is still learning and identifying gaps in her understanding of how abortion, legal or not, is an issue of justice, equity, and equality. But she's not the only *Dirty Dancing* alum out in the streets talking about abortion rights. A month before Roe v. Wade was overturned, Jennifer Grey released her memoir, *Out of the Corner*. It's a genuinely great read and a particularly wonderful listening experience as she narrates the audiobook herself. In it, Grey writes candidly about her own experience of abortion when she was a teenager, as well as the lasting cultural impact of *Dirty Dancing* on abortion discourse. In fact, her interview with the *L.A. Times* to promote her memoir was scheduled the same day the ruling came down and Grey almost cancelled the appointment, explaining, "I feel

---

35 Heather Schwedel, "Movies That Depict Abortion Shouldn't Leave Out the Money Part," *Slate*, May 31, 2022, https://slate.com/culture/2022/05/dirty-dancing-abortion-movies-cost-funding.html.

so emotional. Even though I've seen it coming, even though we've been hearing what's coming, it doesn't feel real."[36]

Grey is still moved by Bergstein's moxie at embedding an illegal abortion so deeply into *Dirty Dancing*'s DNA. "We saw someone who was hemorrhaging. We saw what happens to people without means — the haves and the have-nots. I love that part of the storyline because it was really a feminist movie in a rom-com. It was a perfect use of history." Grey's own abortion story is at times harrowing, especially in hindsight. In *Out of the Corner*, Grey writes about how she was a teenager and living with a man more than a decade older than her, spending her nights at Studio 54 and doing a lot of drugs. "When I try to imagine my own daughter at 16, playing house, essentially living with a grown-ass man, doing tons of blow, popping Quaaludes, and going to Studio — not to mention being lied to, cheated on, then gifted with various and sundry STDs and unwanted pregnancies, it makes me feel physically ill. No teenager should be swimming in waters that dark."[37]

Grey had the means to access abortion, and though she considers it a serious decision that's never left her, she has never regretted her choice. "I wouldn't have my life. I wouldn't have had the career I had, I wouldn't have had anything. And it wasn't for lack of taking it seriously. I'd always wanted a child. I just didn't want a child as a teenager. I didn't want

36 Yvonne Villarreal, "An 'Emotional' Jennifer Grey Opens up about How Abortion Changed Her Life," *Los Angeles Times*, July 14, 2022 https://www.latimes.com/entertainment-arts/books /story/2022-07-14/jennifer-grey-memoir-out-of-the-corner.

37 Jennifer Grey, *Out of the Corner: A Memoir* (New York: Ballantine, 2022).

a child where I was [at] in my life." Grey calls the Supreme Court ruling fundamentally wrong. "It is sounding a bell for all women to rise up and use their voice now because we have assumed, since 1973, that our choice was safe and that it was never going to be overturned."

The overwhelming majority of people in the USA actually support choice;[38] it's a powerful minority that is working overtime to roll back reproductive rights. Bergstein says she has tremendous faith in young people mobilizing to change the world, as well as pop culture's part in political resistance.

> I think popular movies and TV can give you a role model for moral, sensual, sexual, ethical behavior that makes you feel attached to the world. What I hoped for with *Dirty Dancing* was that it would attach [viewers] to the world in a way that brought honor to themselves and to the world. And I think everyone has a secret dancer inside them and such. I think it can and does encourage people to be their best selves, and to think that they can make a difference. And I think that's so important, which is why now I'm concerned with making political action a thing that people want to do. I go to these marches and I give speeches and such, but I think that popular culture will change things more. Or I hope so.[39]

38 Ed Kilgore, "A Majority of Americans Are Pro-Choice, Even in Red States," *New York*, February 23, 2023, https://nymag.com/intelligencer/2023/02/majority-americans-pro-choice-red-states.html.

39 https://www.vice.com/en/article/433a99/the-back-alley-abortion-that-almost-didnt-make-it-into-dirty-dancing

5

Dirty Dancing Forever

When I went away to university, I was nervous and scared, unsure of what this new life would hold. In that first weekend in the dorms, I was keenly aware that this felt like every other first day of school — September's racing heartbeat like an annual drum solo and the new peers and new teachers whose peccadillos and quirks I'd have to observe, manage, and navigate — except we also all lived together. It would have been funnier if I hadn't wanted to throw up. We were teenage strangers in a coed (gender binary firmly in effect) concrete tower, many of us on our own for the first time, trying to figure out who we and our potential friends might be in this completely new setting of relative independence.

We bonded in our shared first-year anxieties and excitements, before a massive cultural moment shocked the world: Princess Diana was killed suddenly in a car accident when the paparazzi chased the vehicle in which she was a passenger. The tragedy was like a shadow all around us the entire weekend, and it guided and shaped our conversations in various ways: those of us who knew grief were talking about her children; there were others who had idolized Diana as the princess they could relate to and aspire to; and all of us were compelled by the macabre and sinister way in which fame had literally killed her. It triggered a global mourning that felt inescapable. By the Monday night of our first weekend, most of us had been in the dorms for two nights and we had already told and then forgotten each other's names once or twice, touched on Diana's shocking death, and shared our majors. Some of us gathered in the TV lounge and started flipping through the channels and, of course, there was *Dirty Dancing*.

It felt like a sign, and many of us let out an involuntary roar of excitement. I can't remember if we tuned in on time for the opening credits, but I do remember that the room eventually filled up with teens from all four floors and, by the time we got to the end of the movie, it was as crowded as the dance floor in the film's opening scene. When Baby finally made the lift, we exploded into cheers. It was our moment as much as her and Johnny's. There isn't any other movie that we could have watched that would have served us better in that moment and in that place. We were all saying goodbye to summer, facing new fears and uncertainties, scared to take the next leap. It was actually ridiculously on the nose, but that's what made it so meaningful. We were on the cusp of something momentous, we didn't have time for subtlety. We needed to watch a young woman take control of her life and fucking nail it. We needed an icon.

My love of *Dirty Dancing* continued, and I was thrilled to share it with my cousin, Kamiko, when the time was right. She's 14 years younger than me and we've been extremely close since she was born. When she was in Grade 5 or 6, I showed her *Dirty Dancing* for the first time. To practice her handwriting, when I was tutoring her, I had her write out the lyrics to "(I've Had) The Time of My Life." To this day, Kam gets dressed up as Baby for annual screenings of *Dirty Dancing* (she owns two different iconic Baby outfits — white Keds, tight white jeans, and white top, as well as denim short shorts and a faded red-orange bodysuit) and even has a watermelon purse just because she's that damn cool and committed.

We are devoted to Baby, we show up for Baby, but that doesn't mean we didn't love Johnny Castle and, of course, the beautiful man who brought him to life, Patrick Swayze.

When Swayze died from pancreatic cancer on September 14, 2009, Kam and I, like probably every *Dirty Dancing* fan, were devastated. What Swayze brought to the screen in *Dirty Dancing* was magic. He took himself seriously and he took dance very seriously, and even though Johnny Castle might be read as an early himbo, Swayze imbues the character with a lot of himself and his own experiences, deliberately and subconsciously. Like Johnny, Swayze was a tough-guy dancer whose soft side was often obscured by other people's projections and assumptions. Swayze wrote poetry and songs and danced professionally for two ballet companies in New

York City, but he also posed nude for cash, taught dance, and fought to make ends meet with woodworking and construction jobs. Swayze's memoir, *The Time of My Life*, co-written with his wife, Lisa Niemi, is a fascinating account of the hundreds of lives he lived in his all-too-short time. He wrote and recorded the book and audiobook after his diagnosis but before he knew his cancer was terminal, and there's something so bittersweet about hearing Swayze's real voice share his own story, knowing now that he passed two weeks before the book's publication on September 29, 2009.

Dirty Dancing's unexpected success made Swayze a star overnight, and he was able to leverage it into a wild few years in Hollywood, making several films including two cult favorites (1989's *Road House* and 1991's *Point Break*) and a genuine box-office blockbuster: 1990's *Ghost*. He was named *People*'s Sexiest Man in 1991 and he continued to have a busy career in Hollywood until his death. All of this was likely thanks to Swayze refusing to participate in a *Dirty Dancing* sequel that some producers wanted to rush into production to capitalize on the massive box office and soundtrack sales. Niemi confirmed his belief that the ending of the original *Dirty Dancing* was "absolutely perfect." Niemi also recalled several iterations of a script for the proposed sequel, "but Patrick had a high standard and he wasn't gonna do it just for the money."[40]

---

40 Callum Crumlish, "Dirty Dancing 2: Jennifer Grey Details Patrick Swayze's 'Tricky' Link to Sequel," *Express*, January 1, 2023, https://www.express.co.uk/entertainment/films/1673296/dirty -dancing-2-patrick-swayze-jennifer-grey-baby-corner-johnny-castle.

Rumors circulated for years about whether there would ever be another *Dirty Dancing*. And then in 2004, there wasn't just one new *Dirty Dancing*. There were two.

A TALE OF TWO *DIRTY DANCING(S)* IN 2004

Five years before Swayze's death, he stepped back into the *Dirty Dancing* extended cinematic universe with a small but thrilling role in *Dirty Dancing: Havana Nights*. He's the highlight of the movie, a kind of baffling adaptation of the original but set in 1950s Cuba, right on the cusp of revolution. I greatly enjoyed Diego Luna as Javier, the Johnny Castle–type role, a waiter in the ritzy hotel catering to rich American visitors, whose family has been devastated by the current fascist regime under Batista. He meets Katey (Romola Garai), the smart and head-strong young, blond Baby stand-in, who is not as vapid and racist as her teenaged American peers. Katey gets a glimpse of Javier dancing amongst "real Cubans" in the streets and she's intrigued. She asks him to be her partner in the New Year's Eve dance competition that will award the winning couple $5,000 and a trip to America, a prize that Javier needs after he's been fired for the crime of walking Katey to her hotel.

The dance scenes are fine, but the actors don't have much chemistry and they're never really believably dancing at a competitive level, even in an amateur competition. But the movie gets a jolt of life when Katey glimpses Swayze's dance instructor character doing what he does best: teaching a room full of women to dance. Swayze has two substantial scenes, both involving him teaching Katey to dance, and it's just a completely different movie in these moments. And it goes beyond the thrill of seeing *the* Johnny Castle in a film partially titled *Dirty Dancing*; it's Swayze at his best, teaching a person to embody their body, to really live inside their body and feel everything without fear, to trust their own vulnerability and their partner.

Bergstein didn't have anything to do with *Havana Nights*. In 2004, she was too busy launching her full-scale musical adaptation, *Dirty Dancing: The Classic Story on Stage*. Bergstein, who wrote the book and used almost all of the same songs (with a couple of additions and notable exceptions, specifically "She's Like the Wind," which is only briefly teased with a few bars of the arrangement when Johnny drives off, leaving the Kellermans and Baby in a cloud of dust), had resisted turning her beloved film into a musical for ages. But two years after the 9/11 attacks, she attended a Bruce Springsteen show at Shea Stadium and felt this overwhelming sense of comfort and solidarity take hold of the audience. It's also one of my favorite things about seeing a show with an audience: we're all totally in the moment, experiencing it together, and the vibe can't help but be joyful, hopeful, and cathartic. Bergstein wanted to create a similar experience for *Dirty Dancing* fans. She wrote quickly and added scenes and story beats, and gave numerous interviews about how the stage adaptation was an opportunity to make the subtle political messaging of the original film more overt with explicit references to war, class, and racism. Baby and Johnny would even argue about voting.[41]

The musical clocks in at about 120 minutes, whereas the movie is just 100. And it's not a traditional musical, either: Baby and Johnny don't break into song at any point. There are singers and a band performing about three quarters of the music live, while other songs are prerecorded and projected in a multimedia experience. For Bergstein, the music and the dancing are what matter, but she doesn't believe that the main dancers (Baby and Johnny) need to be singing to each other, or that they're an impossible aspiration for non-dancing fans. "The whole point of this story is, it can be you," Bergstein told *Backstage* magazine.[42] "It can be anybody. If your heart is high enough, you can dance in a way that transforms your life. It's not really a story about dancers. It's about people who find the power of dance to connect them to the world and their hearts."

The stage production had its world premiere in Australia in 2004 and ticket sales wildly exceeded expectations, even though the reviews were mixed. In 2006, the show made its debut in London's West End and set a sales record for advance tickets. It closed five years later, but it also launched international tours in 2009 in the U.S. and Canada, and has since toured Europe, the U.K., South Africa, Hong Kong, and Singapore. From 2008 to 2020, one of my regular writing gigs was reviewing

---

41 Goldstein.

42 Rachel B. Levin, Still 'Dancing,' *Backstage*, November 5, 2019, https://www.backstage.com/magazine/article/still-dancing-62527/.

theater professionally but somehow I never had the occasion to see *Dirty Dancing* onstage. All that changed on March 27, 2023, when I happened to be in London, England, at the same time as the final few weeks of yet another run of *Dirty Dancing* in London's West End. Almost 20 years after its debut, and six months into the writing of this book, I finally had my chance to see Bergstein's adaptation of her own iconic film.

I tried to remain neutral even as a massively tall vertical LED billboard outside our hotel room on Leicester Square gleamed the production's promotional images straight into our window. White text on a hot pink backdrop read, "'The biggest live theatre sensation of all time' RETURNS 2023!" above a recreation of an indelible image of Baby and Johnny: post-lift but her feet are nowhere near the ground and instead she's still in his arms, his face buried in her torso, her head thrown back in triumph and joy.

I expected a love letter to the film, a victory lap, perhaps, by Bergstein, and her chance to make an even more subversive, feminist, political statement about equality, abortion, and class. What I actually saw was a production that threatens the very legacy of *Dirty Dancing* in its entirety. On the flip side, the stage production makes the film version of *Dirty Dancing* look like an absolute masterpiece for anybody who doubts its value.

The curtain rises and the familiar words of Baby's voice-over from 1987's *Dirty Dancing* practically invite the audience to chime in that she never thought she'd "meet a guy who's as great as my dad." But then a short while later, as talk of the fraught political climate transpires, Baby utters the line, "Shit, I'll die a virgin." This clumsy attempt at edginess is cringeworthy compared to real edginess like making an illegal abortion the heart and soul of the entire plot. The abortion remains, of course, and Marjorie Houseman gets involved, but the script has her treating Baby as a rival for her husband's attention, which feels clichéd and misogynistic. Near the end of the production, after Marjorie comforts her troubled husband and chastises him for keeping secrets from her and risking his medical license (which are valid points), she tells Baby, "I was in love with someone and he left me. And I thought I'd die. But I didn't wreck everyone else's life in the process." YIKES, MOM.

But character assassination as character expansion is part of this iteration of *Dirty Dancing*. Baby and Johnny argue about the Civil Rights Movement, and Johnny is openly racist as he complains that nobody's fighting to help poor white people in his hometown neighborhood. Baby attempts to explain white privilege to him, but, shockingly, she's not outraged or disgusted by his racism. Later, Johnny also participates in a gross bit of sexist, macho posturing about guys getting laid and other sexual clichés that the film's Johnny Castle would never say. Again, Baby isn't turned off or outraged. Jennifer Grey's Baby, the one we fell in love with for her activism and outspokenness, would never have stood for it. Throughout the stage show, Baby calls Johnny on a few things, but the character's fearlessness and intelligence are sacrificed repeatedly.

The most egregious example of this comes at the very end, after the lift (which remains amazing, thank fuck), and after Dr. Houseman has apologized. Baby stares up at Johnny and says (I'm paraphrasing), "They'll say we're too young to know how we really feel. What'll we do then, Johnny?" "We'll fight harder," Johnny replies, repeating a phrase she's said to him at least a few times, essentially stealing and then giving back advice that was hers to begin with. Baby swoons, but I was so enraged I almost lunged out of my side balcony to disrupt the show. So, not only is this not a summer romance, or a story wherein two people grow together, change together, and go on to their own lives, enriched and emboldened by this brief-but-burning-hot August affair, but Baby has to ask Johnny what is possibly the dumbest question of all time? Why doesn't the stage production of *Dirty Dancing* center Baby the way that the film does? Why doesn't Baby get to be the hero of her own story?

I have so many more questions for Bergstein: Why assassinate the characters of Johnny Castle and Baby Houseman? Why make Marjorie so jealous of Baby? Why erase the film's absolutely perfect ending to explicitly keep Baby and Johnny together and give Johnny the last word on their relationship? Why sacrifice Baby's independent spirit? And my most probing/petulant question: How does this 2004 vision of *Dirty Dancing* expand upon the subversive and fiercely feminist spirit of the 1987 film? The only thing it does have going for it? It's marginally better than the most abysmal *Dirty Dancing* adaptation of all time: the 2017 made-for-TV movie.

Bergstein doesn't like *Dirty Dancing* cash grabs. She's spoken at length in numerous interviews about her love for the film's fans and the authenticity of the story. It was why she held off on a sequel for so long, and why she kept saying no to a stage adaptation. So *Dirty Dancing: Havana Nights* and the 2017 *Dirty Dancing* were made without Bergstein. Frankly, the 2017 movie musical makes *Havana Nights* seem almost good. It makes the original *Dirty Dancing* seem like an unimaginable masterpiece of cinema. (And I love the movie. I'm literally writing this book about its genius and influence and you're reading it, but even I'm not saying it's flawless.) The made-for-TV movie is so bad that I now want all of my friends who love *Dirty Dancing* to see it so that we can marvel over the madness that must have gripped the minds of the production team that greenlit this piece of garbage, which so woefully misunderstands its source material that it's almost laughable.

What makes *Dirty Dancing* 2017 such a disaster? Literally almost everything. The casting is awful, and it's a top-down problem starting with leads Colt Prattes as Johnny Castle and Abigail Breslin as Baby. Prattes is a professional dancer, but he's not much of an actor or a singer. Here he tries to do all three at once, while also offering up a pale imitation of Swayze, an expectation that is too much to put on Prattes's shoulders. In a few very quick instances, we get glimpses of Prattes letting down the Johnny mask he seems to think he needs, but he only plays the harsher edges of Johnny's character. He has none of the vulnerability that Swayze brought to the role, a choice that is integral in a feminist coming-of-age film.

Breslin's casting will forever confound me. She's a good actor in other projects, but here it sometimes seems as though she's reading cue cards. In an attempt to "mirror" the original, the producers hired a professional dancer to play Johnny and a non-dancer, Breslin, for Baby. But Grey had taken dance classes at least and loved to dance. Throughout most of the film, Breslin's upper body is so stiff and awkward, I honestly thought she was wearing a back brace. Her top half never connects with her bottom half and there's just no buildup. In the original, we believe Baby is learning to dance, and in part that's what we love about her journey. She steps into herself and frees a part of herself through movement. It honestly doesn't seem like Breslin's Baby actually can dance in either of her big moments.

The screenwriter adapted the story and made attempts to modernize and flesh it out to stretch the one-hundred-minute-minute film into a three-hour made-for-TV musical. In the opening scene, Baby is now reading Betty Friedan's *The Feminine Mystique*, and she and Lisa talk and argue about it at length in the backseat on the ride to Kellerman's. *Do you get it?* the script screams. *Baby is a burgeoning second-wave feminist! Lisa reads magazines and just wants to marry well!* Never mind that Neil Kellerman 2.0 literally has to EXPLAIN the "real" meaning of *The Feminine Mystique* to Baby later in the film and she thanks him, not with a sarcastic sneer but with real sincerity.

The script has zero faith in the actors' abilities to convey anything non-verbal or to trust dancing as a language unto itself. Here are some examples:

- After Baby watches Johnny dance for the first time in the workers' quarters, Billy actually says, "Better change your name, kid, 'cause you're not a baby anymore." It's a gross line, but it's also clunky and unnecessary, which is the ongoing nature of this adaptation.

- When Penny and Baby have a dance lesson together, this is their exchange:

     Penny: "You have to let the man lead . . . There's power in letting go."

     Baby: "I think you're brainwashed."

     Penny: "I think you're too much in your head, Baby. 'Cause dancing comes from down here." [*Penny gestures to her genitals.*]

- Johnny is genuinely cruel to Baby following their first sexual encounter, and Baby is forced to bang on his door and cry that she loves him.

- After Dr. Houseman has saved Penny's life following the botched abortion, which is downplayed significantly in this version, he gives her a patronizing speech about how, after a health scare, it can be a good time to really take a look at your life and your choices.

We also get whole new storylines that mostly fail to reso-
nate: Dr. Houseman (Bruce Greenwood) is now a workaholic
prude who hasn't touched Marjorie (Debra Messing) in over a
year, and she wants a divorce; Vivian Pressman (Katey Sagal) is
a divorced bungalow bunny who performs a fiery rendition of
"Fever" with Johnny but begs him to stay the night after they
have sex because she hates sleeping alone; Lisa (Sara Hyland)
knees Robbie in the groin when he attempts to force himself
on her and then learns the ukulele from Marco (J. Quinton
Johnson), a brilliantly talented young Black musician whom
bandleader Tito (Billy Dee Williams) warns, "Leave the little
white girls alone." Johnson is so talented and charismatic that
it's a relief whenever he's onscreen, but he's just there to give
Lisa a storyline after her assault makes her realize Ivy League
guys like Robbie are entitled predators. Penny's botched abortion story lacks the visceral language and genuine horror of the
original, but singer/actor and former Pussycat Dolls member
Nicole Scherzinger as Penny is the saving grace of this whole
mess. Scherzinger feels like she's in a different movie, a much
better one; she seems to have understood the original's importance and legacy in ways she was genuinely honored to uphold.
Her song and dance numbers are great, she's giving excellent
tough-girl-with-a-tender-heart vibes, and she elevates every
scene she's in.

The script keeps the essence of some of Bergstein's most
iconic lines, but changes them in infuriating ways. "I carried his
watermelon," Baby says, rather than "I carried a watermelon."

At its most extreme reading, the change from "a" to "his" turns Baby into a literal servant of the patriarchy. It can also be read as euphemistic and sexual, again in service to the patriarchy. A language change like this is extremely specific, even if small, and it helps strip away some of Baby's agency, a characteristic of this adaptation. When we finally reach the big finale, Johnny tells Baby, "I had the time of my life with you this summer . . . I love you." But then! Then we flash forward 12 years to the mid-'70s and the opening of the Broadway stage adaptation of Baby's book about that summer at Kellerman's and Johnny is the choreographer of the show. They haven't seen each other since 1963, and we find out Baby is married and a mom to a little girl, and then we get this excruciatingly painful exchange.

Johnny: "You're so fearless. You made me feel I could do anything."
Baby: "That was the summer I stopped being the baby."
Johnny: "Keep on dancin'."
Baby: "You too, Johnny."

Dead. I died. I'm dancing in the great beyond right now as I type this. I have never hated an adaptation more, but now I own it because we had to buy it to watch it and I also want everyone to see it so that they can hate it with me. If I was back in the dorms, this would absolutely be in heavy rotation in the TV lounge. Hate-watching as a group is almost as good as watching something together that everybody truly loves.

The same year that the made-for-TV movie aired, Bergstein wrenched the headlines back in a series of interviews celebrating the film's 30th anniversary. She dropped some honest shade in her assessment of the 2017 remake, telling E! Online that it "isn't the story I would've told." But, she continued, the remake didn't do any lasting damage to the original *Dirty Dancing*. "I was concerned because I was afraid that they would replace the original or turn people against the original, but actually that didn't happen. The *Dirty Dancing* audience is very intuitive and very smart, and so it was fine."[43] Bergstein also casually announced she was finally writing a sequel to *Dirty Dancing*. "The world right after that summer [1963] became very political and chaotic, just like our world now." Bergstein always believed Baby and Johnny had a future, but she wasn't ready to go back into it. "Now I think I am ready to. Partly because it's time, and partly because what happened to them is what's happening now." She believes that contemporary Baby would be an activist supporting women's rights and immigrant rights, and marching for Black Lives Matter.

But Bergstein's vision for Baby (and Johnny) isn't the sequel that's planned for 2024. In fact, Bergstein's sequel doesn't seem to exist, at least as a searchable movie with actual production details behind it. The *Dirty Dancing* sequel that begins filming

---

43 Rebecca Macatee, "*Dirty Dancing* Turns 30: Writer Talks Johnny & Baby's Future, a Possible Sequel & Why Patrick Swayze Was Her First & Only Choice," E!News, August 21, 2017, https://www.eonline.com/news/874313/dirty-dancing-turns-30-writer-talks-johnny-baby -s-future-a-possible-sequel-why-patrick-swayze-was-her-first-only-choice.

in early 2023, however, does star Jennifer Grey (who is also an executive producer) and will be written by Elizabeth Chomko and Jonathan Levine, who is also producing and directing. The film was announced in 2020 and a release date was confirmed in 2022 (the plan, before the months-long 2023 SAG-AFTRA strike, was around Valentine's Day 2024). Grey's involvement is reason to be cautiously optimistic about the sequel. In 2020, she told *Women's Day* about the importance of depicting sexuality, pleasure, satisfaction, and excitement for every age, that rediscovery is not just the domain of youth. Details are slim, but the sequel is set in the 1990s and involves Kellerman's, dancing, music, and romance, and though Grey acknowledges that the success of the first film can't happen again, she's "committed and invested in making it a fresh [take]." But she knows nothing can ever come close to the original. "What happened happened, and that will never happen again," she told *Entertainment Weekly* in an interview about the film's 35th anniversary. "There will never be another Johnny. There will never be another Patrick. This sequel has got to be its own standalone piece. It's very tricky."[44]

In interviews and statements, the men in charge of the sequel keep emphasizing the romance and nostalgia of the original. Lionsgate CEO Jon Feltheimer went so far as to say, in a press release, that this was the kind of film that "the franchise's fans have been waiting for" while co-writer and director Levine issued a statement that read:

---

44 Kristen Baldwin," Dirty Dancing's Jennifer Grey on the Enduring Relatability of 'I carried a watermelon,'" *Entertainment Weekly*, August 19, 2022, https://ew.com/movies/dirty-dancing -35th-anniversary-jennifer-grey-interview-abortion/.

While the original *Dirty Dancing* has always been one of my favorite films, I never imagined I would direct the sequel. Through co-writing it, I fell in love with the characters (new and old), the world of 1990s Catskills New York, and the music, which will range from songs from the original movie to '90s hip-hop. I can't wait to collaborate with Jennifer to bring this beautiful story of summer and romance and dancing to a generation of new fans. And to the longtime ones, I promise we will not ruin your childhood. We will tackle the assignment with sophistication, ambition, and, above all, love.[45]

But *Dirty Dancing* wasn't just a movie where we watched Baby and Johnny fall in love. It radicalized generations of us, made us more socially and politically aware, and it modeled feminist practices of care. It made vulnerability a human trait, not something to reinforce gender stereotypes, and it illustrated what real strength and character could look like in standing up for ourselves and against injustice. Bergstein wrapped her politics inside a sexy, sweet, endearing love story, but she never, ever forgot that Baby is the agent of change, Baby is the hero, and this is Baby's coming-of-age story first and foremost. In fact, for Bergstein, one of the most important scenes in the film actually reinforces the relationship between passion, political change, and the sexual fireworks that stem from that possibility, that feeling of empowerment. Johnny

45 https://deadline.com/2022/05/dirty-dancing-sequel-details-revealed-jonathan-levine-jennifer-grey-music-patrick-swayze-1235019230/

tells Baby, "I've never met anybody like you. You look at the world and you think you can make it better . . . You're not scared of anything." Baby looks at him, incredulous. "I'm scared of walking out of this room and never feeling the rest of my whole life the way I feel when I'm with you!" Then we have the genuinely steamy dance that doubles as foreplay for their first night together. "What I would like to do is get young people to understand that the most exciting, most sexual, most alive thing you can do is to be very, very active in politics," Bergstein told *Tablet Magazine*. "I think that's the only thing that will turn the world around in the way it needs to be."[46]

But the exchange between Baby and Johnny, Bergstein told *Bustle*, is ultimately the moral of the film. "At every moment in your life, you have to judge whether you're making the bravest and most honorable decision. If you didn't, you'll look back at it forever, and if you did, whatever happens from it you will feel that you did your best. I think that's what everyone, men, women and kids, react to the most. There is one moment in your life when you have a shot at living your life fully, being entirely in the moment, and either you're brave enough to walk towards it or you're not."[47]

I'm holding out hope for Levine's *Dirty Dancing* sequel. He actually wrote and directed one of my favorite contemporary Christmas movies, *The Night Before*, a funny film that also

46 Aroesty.

47 Sydney Bucksbaum, "'Dirty Dancing' Creator on That Unforgettable Lift," *Bustle*, February 6, 2017, https://www.bustle.com/p/dirty-dancing-creator-on-the-epic-dance-move-that-inspired-countless-reenactments-35542.

does a decent job exploring the growing pains between three men in their early 30s as they attempt to hold onto their friend traditions even as their lives go in separate directions. Levine's musical vision for the sequel is also intriguing. He has gone on the record promising another multi-decade soundtrack that will likely include not just '90s hip-hop, but Alanis Morissette, Liz Phair, and, specifically, "Hungry Eyes." This is another detail that gives me pause, but at least it's a better song than "Overload."

No matter what happens with sequels and adaptations, future remakes and possible prequels, the magic and momentum and authenticity of the original *Dirty Dancing* endures as a subversive, feminist, fun piece of filmmaking that was ahead of its time (and remains timeless) in many ways. It is powerfully resonant and relevant now in a regressive post-Roe landscape where abortion is no longer a constitutional right for all Americans and has been recriminalized in certain states.

Dirty Dancing lives on in the cultural zeitgeist. There are whole tourism industries built around the filming locations, including Lake Lure's annual *Dirty Dancing* Festival, which includes a lake-lift competition, watermelon-related events, dance competitions, costumes, and a screening of the film. The *New York Times* reported that the 2016 festival saw more than two thousand people in attendance.[48] The iconic lift is a

---

48 Neil Genzlinger, "'Dirty Dancing': Where Kellerman's Comes to Life," *New York Times*, May 26, 2015, https://www.nytimes.com/2017/05/26/travel/footsteps-dirty-dancing-movie-30th-anniversary.html.

wildly risky dance move performed at wedding receptions as "(I've Had) The Time of My Life" blares in the background. "I carried a watermelon" and "Nobody puts Baby in a corner" have been referenced in books, movies, TV shows, and other media. *Dirty Dancing* reality television competition shows have popped up around the world. From 2007's *Dirty Dancing: The Time of Your Life*, where British dancers traveled to America to stay at the Mountain Lake resort in Virginia and competed weekly for a chance to sign a dance contract with an LA-based company, to 2019's *The Real Dirty Dancing*, an Australian talent show that followed local celebrities as they visited key locations to recreate iconic moments from the original film, which was then adapted into an American version in 2022.

And it all began with a former teenage mambo queen who loved to dance and who believed stories about girls and women were stories worth telling. "I didn't want money, I didn't want fame," Bergstein says in *The Movies That Made Us*. "I wanted my work to change people's lives. I can stand up almost any place in the world and say, 'How many people in this room have seen *Dirty Dancing*?' and almost all of them not only will have, but it means something personal to them. And that's extraordinary. Extraordinary."[49]

Extraordinary is the perfect word to describe *Dirty Dancing*'s reach, its resonance, and its influence. I've tried to channel Baby in so many ways in my life, and she's helped inform my own desire to stand up against injustice and help people while still

---

49 *The Movies That Made Us.*

having boundaries and a strong belief in my own worth. Baby was a starting point, and not without her flaws, but she truly helped me think about what it is to be brave and all the different ways it could look. It might mean pushing myself to try something I've never done, or taking a risk and telling someone how I felt, or telling the truth no matter what. Like Baby, I grew up wanting to change the world. But *Dirty Dancing* showed me, through Baby, that it's really about *helping* change the world. Helping change the world — to make it a more just, inclusive, and equitable place for everyone — starts with community care and radiates out. *Dirty Dancing* shows us that our communities are dynamic and not always made up of relations or peers: Penny's community suddenly includes Baby and Dr. Houseman; Baby's community expands to include Johnny and Penny and all of the dancers, collapsing the class barriers between them, even if temporarily.

Dirty Dancing also shows up in my relationship to my body. I am very aware that there are no fat dancers in *Dirty Dancing*. In fact, the only fat actor is Wayne Knight as the mildly annoying Kellerman's social director, Stan. But I am very used to a lack of fulsome representation when it comes to fat bodies on big and small screens. But it didn't mean that I didn't relate to Baby's desire to learn to dance and embody her form fully and completely. More than 35 years after first watching the film, I am still trying to live in my body in a way that feels truly empowered and free, where I feel strong and sexy and alive. I was surrounded by a lot of anti-fatness most of my life and it takes a long time to unlearn it, even if I am routinely overly or even deservedly confident in many other areas. The pandemic shrunk me and made me scared and anxious and stiff in ways that will take me years to fully understand and heal from, but thinking about *Dirty Dancing* so deeply and for so long while writing this book has reminded me of how much joy there is in movement. I love to dance. I'm mostly terrible at it, but I absolutely love it.

Above all else, in making *Dirty Dancing* with as much care, intention, and deliberate subversiveness as she did, Eleanor Bergstein helped change my life and the lives of millions of fans. Baby, Penny, Lisa, and Bergstein echo in the pop culture that's shaped my feminism, interests, morals, ethics, friendships, humor, musical tastes, and purpose. I'm also in awe of Bergstein's dedication to her vision for *Dirty Dancing*, and what she refused to give up. She was a writer without a proven track record, but she was unshakeable in her belief in Baby and, frankly, herself. More than 40 rejections from studios: that was the beginning of *Dirty Dancing*, and Bergstein never forgets it. Her advice to other writers? "Just pick yourself up off the floor again, and again, again, and again. Something that is enormously popular seems inevitable but it never is. The only way it will be inevitable is if it's a copy of something that's been done before and who wants to do that? If it's something nobody has done before you'll get a lot of pushback and misery. Staying power is all. I will be indefatigable, sit in the face of scorn, I will fight."[50] That is my *Dirty Dancing*.

50 Shanee Edwards, "9 Big Takeaways from Dirty Dancing Screenwriter Eleanor Bergstein," *Screencraft*, December 12, 2018, https://screencraft.org/blog/9-big-takeaways-from-dirty-dancing -screenwriter-eleanor-bergstein/.

Acknowledgments

It takes so many people to publish a book and this is a celebration of all of those people!

Thank you to Jen Sookfong Lee, who is a wild, generous genius. She's such a tremendous writer and also a brilliant editor and co-conspirator and I feel so lucky to work with her. It's like being chosen by the coolest person to be part of the best team and I'm so grateful to Jen for her encouragement and support. Thank you to everyone at ECW, especially Jen Knoch, Anita Ragunathan, Shannon Parr, Michela Prefontaine, Emily Ferko, Jessica Albert, Victoria Cozza, Emily Varsava, Lisa Frenette, and Jack David. Thank you to Hannah McGregor for inspiring me to pitch this book. I cannot wait to be Pop Classic peers with Hannah when *Clever Girl* is published in Fall 2024.

Thank you to Carlos Hernandez Fisher, Cynara Geissler, and Holly Gordon for reading early drafts of this book and encouraging me to think more deeply about myself, the film, and the world. I am so grateful for their beautiful brains and faces, that they take this movie as seriously as I do, and for making the feedback and editing process so rich and rewarding. I love them all very much.

Thank you to my agent, Carolyn Forde, who said yes to a cold-call coffee invitation and has been making my life better ever since. I'm so lucky to have her in my corner and I'm thrilled to be working with her. Thank you to my colleagues at CBC Music for making me a better writer and thinker, and to all of the editors I've worked with over the years.

Thank you to the family, friends, and loved ones past and present who have watched/talked/argued/discussed/debated/shared with/indulged me in my love of *Dirty Dancing*, especially Jenn, Kamiko, and Julia, who have all consumed this movie with me at extremely important milestones throughout our lives.

Thank you to everyone involved in the creation of *Dirty Dancing* for making a movie (and soundtrack) that's meant so much to so many of us, and quietly radicalized generations of young, horny feminists who love music and moving our bodies and who believe abortion is healthcare. And thank you to the people on the ground, in the streets, at the non-profits and the clinics, in the hospitals, and in the courthouses who are all striving to ensure barrier-free, safe, and legal reproductive healthcare for everyone. Justice for Penny, justice for all.

Andrea Warner is a settler who lives in Vancouver on the unceded territories of the Musqueam, Squamish, and Tsleil-Waututh First Nations. Her books include *Rise Up and Sing!: Power, Protest, and Activism in Music* and *Buffy Sainte-Marie: The Authorized Biography*. Andrea is the co-writer and associate producer of the documentary *Buffy Sainte-Marie: Carry It On* and the co-host of the weekly feminist pop culture podcast, *Pop This!*

This book is also available as a Global Certified Accessible™ (GCA) ebook. ECW Press's ebooks are screen reader friendly and are built to meet the needs of those who are unable to read standard print due to blindness, low vision, dyslexia, or a physical disability.

At ECW Press, we want you to enjoy our books in whatever format you like. If you've bought a print copy or an audiobook not purchased with a subscription credit, just send an email to ebook@ecwpress.com and include:

- the book title
- the name of the store where you purchased it
- a screenshot or picture of your order/receipt number and your name

A real person will respond to your email with your ePub attached. If you prefer to receive the ebook in PDF format, please let us know in your email.

Some restrictions apply. This offer is only valid for books already available in the ePub format. Some ECW Press books do not have an ePub format for us to send you. In those cases, we will let you know if a PDF format is available as an alternative. This offer is only valid for books purchased for personal use. At this time, this program is not offered on school or library copies.

Thank you for supporting an independently owned Canadian publisher with your purchase!